THE GREAT
HERESIES

THE GREAT HERESIES

By

Hilaire Belloc

TAN BOOKS AND PUBLISHERS, INC.
Rockford, Illinois 61105

First published in 1938 by Sheed & Ward, London.

Retypeset and republished in 1991 by TAN Books and Publishers, Inc.

ISBN: 0-89555-475-5

Library of Congress Catalog Card No.: 91-66422

Printed and bound in the United States of America.

TAN BOOKS AND PUBLISHERS, INC.
P.O. Box 424
Rockford, Illinois 61105

1991

To

REGINALD JEBB

TABLE OF CONTENTS

THE GREAT HERESIES

1

HERESY

What is a heresy, and what is the historical importance of such a thing?

Like most modern words, "Heresy" is used both vaguely and diversely. It is used vaguely because the modern mind is as averse to precision in ideas as it is enamored of precision in measurement. It is used diversely because, according to the man who uses it, it may represent any one of fifty things.

Today, with most people (of those who use the English language), the word "Heresy" connotes bygone and forgotten quarrels, an old prejudice against rational examination. Heresy is therefore thought to be of no contemporary interest. Interest in it is dead, because it deals with matter no one now takes seriously. It is understood that a man may interest himself in a heresy from archaeological curiosity, but if he affirm that it has been of great effect on history and still is, today, of living contemporary moment, he will be hardly understood.

Yet the subject of heresy in general is of the highest importance to the individual and to society, and heresy in its particular meaning (which is that of heresy in Christian doctrine) is of special interest for anyone who would understand Europe: the character of Europe and the story of Europe. For the whole of that story, since the appearance of the Christian religion, has been the story of struggle and change, mainly preceded by, often, if not always, caused by, and certainly accompanying, diversities of religious doctrine. In other words, "the Christian heresy" is a special subject of the very first importance to the comprehension of European history, because, in company with Christian orthodoxy, it is the constant accompaniment and agent of European life.

We must begin by a definition, although definition involves a mental effort and therefore repels.

Heresy is the dislocation of some complete and self-supporting scheme by the introduction of a novel denial of some essential part therein.

We mean by "a complete and self-supporting scheme" any system of affirmation in physics or mathematics or philosophy or what-not, the various parts of which are coherent and sustain each other.

For instance, the old scheme of physics, often called in England, "Newtonian" as having been best defined by Newton, is a scheme of this kind. The various things asserted therein about the behavior of matter, notably the law of gravity, are not isolated statements any one of which could be withdrawn at will without disarranging the rest; they are all parts of one conception, or unity, such that if you but modify a part the whole scheme is put out of gear.

Another example of a similar system is our plane geometry, inherited through the Greeks and called by those who think (or hope) they have got hold of a new geometry "Euclidean." Every proposition in our plane geometry—that the internal angles of a plane triangle equal two right angles, that the angle contained in a semi-circle is a right angle, and so forth—is not only sustained by every other proposition in the scheme, but in its turn supports each other individual part of the whole.

Heresy means, then, the warping of a system by "Exception": by "Picking out" one part of the structure[1] and implies that the scheme is marred by taking away one part of it, denying one part of it, and either leaving the void unfilled or filling it with some new affirmation. For instance, the nineteenth century completed a scheme of textual criticism for establishing the date of an ancient document. One of the principles in this scheme is

---

1. The word is derived from the Greek verb *Haireo,* which first meant "I grasp" or "I seize," and then came to mean "I take away."

this—that any statement of the marvelous is necessarily false. 'When you find in any document a marvel, vouched for by the supposed author of that document, you have a right to conclude" (say the textual critics of the nineteenth century, all talking like one man) "that the document was not contemporary—was not of the date which it is claimed to be." There comes along a new and original critic who says, "I don't agree. I think that marvels happen and I also think that people tell lies." A man thus butting in is a heretic in relation to that particular orthodox system. Once you grant this exception a number of secure negatives become insecure.

You were certain, for instance, that the life of St. Martin of Tours, which professed to be by a contemporary witness, was not by a contemporary witness because of the marvels it recited. But if the new principle be admitted, it might be contemporary after all, and therefore something to which it bore witness, in no way marvelous but not found in any other document, may be accepted as historical.

You read in the life of a Thaumaturge that he raised a man from the dead in the basilica of Vienna in A.D. 500. The orthodox school of criticism would say that the whole story being obviously false, because marvelous, it is no evidence for the existence of a basilica in Vienna at that date. But your heretic, who disputes the orthodox canon of criticism, says, "It seems to me that the biographer of the Thaumaturge may have been telling lies, but that he would not have mentioned the basilica and the date unless contemporaries knew, as well as he did, that there *was* a basilica in Vienna at that date. *One* falsehood does not presuppose *universal* falsehood in a narrator." There might even come along a still bolder heretic who should say, "Not only is this passage perfectly good evidence for the existence of a basilica at Vienna in A.D. 500, but I think it possible that the man *was* raised from the dead." If you follow either of these critics you are upsetting a whole scheme of tests, whereby true history was sifted from false in the textual criticism of recent times.

The denial of a scheme wholesale is not heresy, and has not the creative power of a heresy. It is of the essence of heresy that it leaves standing a great part of the structure it attacks. On this account it can appeal to believers and continues to affect their lives through deflecting them from their original characters. Wherefore it is said of heresies that "they survive by the truths they retain."

We most note that whether the complete scheme thus attacked be true or false is indifferent to the value of heresy as a department of historical study. What we are concerned with is the highly interesting truth that heresy originates a new life of its own and vitally affects the society it attacks. The reason that men combat heresy is not only, or principally, conservatism—a devotion to routine, a dislike of disturbance in their habits of thought—it is much more a perception that the heresy, insofar as it gains ground, will produce a way of living and a social character at issue with, irritating, and perhaps mortal to, the way of living and the social character produced by the old orthodox scheme.

So much for the general meaning and interest of that most pregnant word "Heresy."

Its particular meaning (the meaning in which it is used in this book) is the marring by exception of that complete scheme, the Christian religion.

For instance, that religion has for one essential part (though it is only a part) the statement that the individual soul is immortal—that personal conscience survives physical death. Now if people believe that, they look at the world and themselves in a certain way and go on in a certain way and are people of a certain sort. If they except, that is cut out, this one doctrine, they may continue to hold all the others, but the scheme is changed, the type of life and character and the rest become quite other. The man who is certain that he is going to die for good and all may believe that Jesus of Nazareth was Very God of Very God, that God is Triune, that the Incarnation was accompanied by a Virgin Birth, that bread and wine are transformed by a particular formula; he may recite a great number of Christian prayers and admire and copy chosen Christian exemplars, but he will be quite a different man from the man who takes immortality for granted.

Because heresy, in this particular sense (the denial of an accepted Christian doctrine) thus affects the individual, it affects all society, and when you are examining a society formed by a particular religion you necessarily concern yourself to the utmost with the warping or diminishing of that religion. *That is the historical interest of heresy. That* is why anyone who wants to understand how Europe came to be, and how its changes have been caused, cannot afford to treat heresy as unimportant. The ecclesiastics who fought so furiously over the details of definition in the Eastern councils had far more historical sense and were far more in touch with reality than the French skeptics, familiar to English readers through their disciple Gibbon.

A man who thinks, for instance, that Arianism is a mere discussion of words, does not see that an Arian world would have been much more like a Mohammedan world than what the European world actually became. He is much less in touch with reality than was Athanasius when he affirmed the point of doctrine to be all-important. That local council in Paris, which tipped the scale in favor of the Trinitarian tradition, was of as much effect as a decisive battle, and not to understand that is to be a poor historian.

It is no answer to such a thesis to say that both the orthodox and the heretic were suffering from illusion, that they were discussing matters which had no real existence and were not worth the trouble of debate. The point is that the doctrine (and its denial) were formative of the nature of men, and the nature so formed determined the future of the society made up of those men.

There is another consideration in this connection which is too often omitted in our time. It is this: That the skeptical attitude upon transcendental things cannot, for masses of men, endure. It has been the despair of many that this should be so. They deplore the despicable weakness of mankind which compels the acceptation of some philosophy or some religion in order to carry on life at all. But we have here a matter of positive and universal experience.

Indeed there is no denying it. It is mere fact. Human society cannot carry on without some creed, because a code and a character are the product of a creed. In point of fact though individuals, especially those who have led sheltered lives, can often carry on with a minimum of certitude or habit upon transcendental things, an organic human mass cannot so carry on. Thus a whole religion sustains modern England, the religion of patriotism. Destroy that in men by some heretical development, by "excepting" the doctrine that a man's prime duty is towards the political society to which he belongs, and England, as we know it, would gradually cease and become something other.

Heresy, then, is not a fossil subject. It is a subject of permanent and vital interest to mankind because it is bound up with the subject of religion, without some form of which no human society ever has endured, or ever can endure. Those who think that the subject of heresy may be neglected because the term sounds to them old-fashioned and because it is connected with a number of disputes long abandoned, are making the common error of thinking in words instead of ideas. It is the same sort of error which contrasts America as a "republic" with England as a "monarchy," whereas, of course, the Government of the United States is essentially monarchic and the Government of England essentially republican and aristocratic. There is no end to the misunderstandings which arise from the uncertain use of words. But if we keep in mind the plain fact that a state, a human polity, or a general culture, must be inspired by some body of morals, and that there can be no body of morals without doctrine, and if we agree to call any consistent body of morals and doctrine a religion, then the importance of heresy as a subject will be clear, because heresy means nothing else than "the proposal of novelties in religion by picking out from what has been the accepted religion some point or other, denying the same or replacing it by another doctrine hitherto unfamiliar."

The study of successive Christian heresies, their characters and fates, has a special interest for all of us who belong to the European or Christian culture, and that is a reason that ought to be self-evident—our culture was made by a religion. Changes in, or deflections from, that religion necessarily affect our civilization as a whole.

The whole story of Europe, her various realms and states and general body during the last sixteen centuries has mainly turned upon the successive heresies arising in the Christian world.

We are what we are today mainly because no one of those heresies finally overset our ancestral religion, but we also are what we are because each of them profoundly affected our fathers for generations, each heresy left behind it traces, and one of them, the great Mohammedan movement, remains to this day in dogmatic force and preponderant over a great fraction of territory which was once wholly ours.

If one were to catalogue heresies, marking the whole long story of Christendom, the list would seem almost endless. They divide and subdivide, they are on every scale, they vary from the local to the general. Their lives extend from less than a generation to centuries. The best way of understanding the subject is to select a few prominent examples, and by the study of these to understand of what vast import heresy may be.

Such a study is the easier from the fact that our fathers recognized heresy for what it was, gave it in each case a particular name, subjected it to definition and therefore to limits, and made its analysis the easier by such definition.

Unfortunately in the modern world the habit of such definition has been lost; the word "heresy" having come to connote something odd and old-fashioned, is no longer applied to cases which are clearly cases of heresy and ought to be treated as such.

For instance, there is abroad today a denial of what theologians call "dominion"—that is the right to own property. It is widely affirmed that laws permitting the private ownership of land and capital are immoral; that the soil and all goods which are productive should be communal and that any system leaving their control to individuals or families is wrong and therefore to be attacked and destroyed.

That doctrine, already very strong among us and increasing in strength and the number of its adherents, we do not call a heresy. We think of it only as a political or economic system, and when we speak of Communism our vocabulary does not suggest anything theological. But this is only because we have forgotten what the word theological means. Communism is as much a heresy as Manichaeism. It is the taking away from the moral scheme by which we have lived of a particular part, the denial of that part and the attempt to replace it by an innovation. The Communist retains much of the Christian scheme—human equality, the right to live, and so forth—he denies a *part* of it only.

The same is true of the attack on the indissolubility of marriage. No one calls the mass of modern practice and affirmation upon divorce a heresy, but a heresy it clearly is because its determining characteristic is the denial of the Christian doctrine of marriage and the substitution therefore of another doctrine, to wit, that marriage is but a contract, and a terminable contract.

Equally is it a heresy, a "change by exception," to affirm that nothing can be known upon divine things, that all is mere opinion and that therefore things made certain by the evidence of the senses and by experiment should be our only guides in arranging human affairs. Those who think thus may and commonly do retain much of Christian morals, but because they deny certitude from Authority, which doctrine is a part of Christian epistemology, they are heretical. It is not heresy to say that reality can be reached by experiment, by sensual perception and by deduction. It *is* heresy to say that reality can be attained from no other source.

We are living today under a regime of heresy with only this to distinguish it from the older periods of heresy, that the heretical spirit has become generalized and appears in various forms.

It will be seen that I have, in the following pages, talked of "the modern attack" because some name must be given to a thing before one can discuss it at all, but the tide which threatens to overwhelm us is so diffuse that each must give it his own name; it has no common name as yet.

Perhaps that will come, but not until the conflict between the modern anti-Christian spirit and the permanent tradition of the Faith becomes acute through persecution and the triumph or defeat thereof. It will then perhaps be called Anti-Christ.

2

SCHEME OF THIS BOOK

I propose in what follows to deal with the main attacks upon the Catholic Church which have marked her long history. In the case of all but the Moslem and the modern confused but ubiquitous attack, which is still in progress, I deal with their failure and the causes of their failure. I shall conclude by discussing the chances of the present struggle for the survival of the Church in that very civilization which she created and which is now generally abandoning her.

There is, as everybody knows, an institution proclaiming itself today the sole authoritative and divinely appointed teacher of essential morals and essential doctrine. This institution calls itself the Catholic Church.

It is further an admitted historical truth, which no one denies, that such an institution putting forth such a claim has been present among mankind for very many centuries. Many, through antagonism or lack of knowledge, deny the identity of the Catholic Church today with the original Christian society. No one, however hostile or uninstructed, will deny its presence during at least thirteen or fourteen hundred years.

It is further historically true (though not universally admitted) that the claim of this body to be a divinely appointed voice for the statement of true doctrine on the matters essential to man (his nature, his ordeal in this world, his doom or salvation, his immortality, etc.) is to be found affirmed through preceding centuries, up to a little before the middle of the first century.

From the day of Pentecost (some time between A.D. 29 and A.D. 33) onwards there has been a body of doctrine affirmed—

9

for instance, at the very outset, the Resurrection. And the organism by which that body of doctrine has been affirmed has been from the outset a body of men bound by a certain tradition through which they claimed to have the authority in question.

Here we distinguish between two conceptions totally different, which are nevertheless often confused. One is the historical fact that the claim to Divine authority and Infallible doctrine was and is still made; the other the credibility of that claim.

Whether the claim be true or false has nothing whatever to do with its historical origin and continuity; it may have arisen as an illusion or an imposture; it may have been continued in ignorance; but that does not affect its historical existence. The claim has been made and continues to be made, and those who made it are in unbroken continuity with those who made it in the beginning. They form, collectively, the organism which called itself and still calls itself "The Church."

Now against this authoritative organism, its claim, character and doctrines, there have been throughout the whole period of its existence continued assaults. There have been denials of its claim. There have been denials of this or that section of its doctrines. There has been the attempted replacing of these by other doctrines. Even attempted destruction of the organism, the Church, has repeatedly taken place.

I propose to select five main attacks of this kind from the whole of the very great—the almost unlimited—number of efforts, major and minor, to bring down the edifice of unity and authority.

My reason for choosing so small a number as five, and concentrating upon each as a separate phenomenon, is not only the necessity for a framework and for limits, but also the fact that in these five the main forms of attack are exemplified. These five are, in their historical order, 1. The Arian; 2. The Mohammedan; 3. The Albigensian; 4. The Protestant; 5. One to which no specific name has as yet been attached, but which we shall call for the sake of convenience "the Modern."

I say that each of these five main campaigns, the full success of any one of which would have involved the destruction of the

Catholic Church, its authority and doctrine among men, presents a type.

The Arian attack proposed a change of fundamental doctrine, such that, had the change prevailed, the whole nature of the religion would have been transformed. It would not only have been transformed, it would have failed; and with its failure would have followed the breakdown of that civilization which the Catholic Church was to build up.

The Arian heresy (filling the fourth, and active throughout the fifth, century), proposed to go to the very root of the Church's authority by attacking the full Divinity of her Founder. But it did much more, because its underlying motive was a rationalizing of the mystery upon which the Church bases herself: the mystery of the Incarnation. Arianism was essentially a revolt against the difficulties attaching to mysteries as a whole though expressing itself as an attack on the chief mystery only. Arianism was a typical example on the largest scale of that reaction against the supernatural which, when it is fully developed, withdraws from religion all that by which religion lives.

The Mohammedan attack was of a different kind. It came geographically from just outside the area of Christendom; it appeared, almost from the outset, as a foreign enemy; yet was it not, strictly speaking, a new religion attacking the old, it was essentially a heresy; but from the circumstances of its birth it was a heresy alien rather than intimate. It threatened to kill the Christian Church by invasion rather than to undermine it from within.

The Albigensian attack was but the chief of a great number, all of which drew their source from the Manichean conception of a duality in the Universe; the conception that good and evil are ever struggling as equals, and that Omnipotent Power is neither single nor beneficent. Closely intertwined with this idea and inseparable from it was the conception that matter is evil and that all pleasure, especially of the body, is evil. This form of attack, of which I say the Albigensian was the most notorious and came nearest to success, was rather an attack upon morals than upon doctrine; it had the character of a cancer fastening upon the body of the Church from within, producing a new life of its own, antagonistic to the life of the Church and destructive of it—just as a malignant growth in the human body lives a life of its own, other than, and destructive of, the organism in which it has parasitically arisen.

The Protestant attack differed from the rest especially in this characteristic, that its attack did not consist in the promulgation of a new doctrine or of a new authority, that it made no concerted attempt at creating a counter-Church, but had for its principle the denial of unity. It was an effort to promote that state of mind in which a *Church* in the old sense of the word—that is, an infallible, united, teaching body, a Person speaking with Divine authority—should be denied; not the doctrines it might happen to advance, but its very claim to advance them with unique authority. Thus, one Protestant may affirm, as do the English Puseyites, the truth of all the doctrines underlying the Mass—the Real Presence, the Sacrifice, the sacerdotal power of consecration, etc.—another Protestant may affirm that all such conceptions are false, yet both these Protestants are Protestant because they communicate in the fundamental conception that the Church is not a visible, definable and united personality, that there is no central infallible authority, and that therefore each is free to choose his own set of doctrines.

Such affirmations of disunion, such denial of the claim to unity as being part of the Divine order, produced indeed a common Protestant temperament through certain historical associations; but there is no one doctrine nor set of doctrines which can be affirmed as being the kernel of Protestantism. Its essential remains the rejection of unity through authority.

Lastly there is that contemporary attack on the Catholic Church which is still in progress and to which no name has been finally attached, save the vague term "modern." I should have preferred, perhaps, the old Greek word, "*alogos*"; but that would have seemed pedantic. And yet it is a pity to have to reject it, for it admirably describes by implication the quarrel between the present attackers of Catholic authority and doctrine, and the tone of mind of a believer. Antiquity began by giving the name *"alogos"* to those who belittled or denied, though calling themselves Christians, the Divinity of Christ. They were said to do so from lack of "wit," in the sense of "fullness of comprehension," "largeness of apprehension." Men felt about this kind of rationalism as normal people feel about a color-blind man.

One might also have chosen the term "Positivism," seeing that the modern movement relies upon the distinction between things positively proved by experiment and things accepted upon other grounds; but the term "Positivism" has already a special connotation and to use it would have been confusing.

At any rate, though we have as yet perhaps no specific name, we all know the spirit to which I refer: "That only is true which can be appreciated by the senses and subjected to experiment. That can most thoroughly be believed which can most thoroughly be measured and tested by repeated trial. What are generally called "religious affirmations" are, always *presumably,* sometimes *demonstrably,* illusions. The idea of God itself and all that follows on it is man-made and a figment of the imagination. This is the attack which has superseded all the older ones, which is now gaining ground so rapidly and whose votaries feel (as did in their hey-day all the votaries of the earlier attacks) an increasing confidence of success.

Such are the five great movements antagonistic to the Faith. To concentrate our attention upon each in turn teaches us in separate examples the character of our religion and the strange truth that men cannot escape sympathy with it or hatred of it.

To concentrate on these five main attacks has this further value, that between them they seem to sum up all the directions from which assault can be delivered against the Catholic Faith.

Doubtless in the future there will be further conflict, indeed we can be sure that it is inevitable, for it is the nature of the Church to provoke the anger and attack of the world. Perhaps we shall have later to meet the heathen from the East, or perhaps, earlier or later, the challenge of a new system altogether—not a heresy but a new religion. But the main *kinds* of attack would seem to be exhausted by the list which history has hitherto presented. We have had examples of heresy, working from without and forming a new world in that fashion, of which Islam is the great example. We have had examples of heresy at work attacking the root of the Faith, the Incarnation, and specializing upon that—of which Arianism was the great example. We have had the growth of the foreign body from within, the Albigenses, and all their Manichean kindred before and after them. We have had the attack on the personality, that is the unity, of the Church—which is Protestantism. And we now behold, even as Protestantism is dying, the rise and growth of yet another form of conflict—the proposal to treat all transcendental affirmation as illusion. It would seem as though the future could hold no more than the repetition of these forms.

The Church might thus be regarded as a citadel presenting a certain number of faces between the angles of its defenses, each face attacked in turn, and after the failure of one attack its neighbor suffering the brunt of the battle. The last assault, the modern one, is more like an attempt to dissolve the garrison, the annihilation of its powers of resistance by suggestion, than an armed conflict. With this last form the list would seem exhausted. If or when the last danger is dissipated, the next can only appear after some fashion of which we have already had experience.

I may be asked by way of postscript to this prelude why I have not included any mention of the schisms. The schisms are as much attacks upon the life of the Catholic Church as are the heresies; the greatest schism of all, the Greek or Orthodox, which has produced the Greek or Orthodox communion, is manifestly a disruption of our strength. Yet I think that the various forms of attack upon the Church by way of heretical doctrine are in a different category from the schisms. No doubt a schism commonly includes a heresy, and no doubt certain heresies have attempted to plead that we should be reconciled with them, as we might be with a schism. But though the two evils commonly appear in company, yet each is of a separate sort from the other;

and as we are studying the one, it is best to eliminate the other during the process of that study.

I shall then in these pages examine in turn the five great movements I have mentioned, and I will take them in historical order, beginning with the Arian business—which, as it was the first, was also, perhaps, the most formidable.

3

THE ARIAN HERESY

Arianism was the first of the great heresies.

There had been from the foundation of the Church at Pentecost A.D. 29² to 33 a mass of heretical movements filling the first three centuries. They had turned, nearly all of them, upon the nature of Christ.

The effect of Our Lord's predication, and Personality, and miracles, but most of all of His resurrection, had been to move everyone who had any faith at all in the wonder presented, to a conception of divine power running through the whole affair.

Now the central tradition of the Church here, as in every other case of disputed doctrine, was strong and clear from the beginning. Our Lord was undoubtedly a man. He had been born as men are born, He died as men die. He lived as a man and had been known as a man by a group of close companions and a very large number of men and women who had followed Him, and heard Him and witnessed His actions.

But—said the Church—He was also *God*. God had come down to earth and had become Incarnate as a Man. He was not merely a man influenced by the Divinity, nor was He a Manifestation of the Divinity under the appearance of a man. He was at the

---

2. For the discussion on the date of the Crucifixion, Resurrection and Pentecost I must refer my readers to Dr. Arendzen's clear and learned work, *Men and Manners in the Time of Christ* (Sheed and Ward). From the evidence, which has been fully examined, it is clear that the date is not earlier than 29 A.D., and may possibly be a few years later, while the most widely accepted traditional date is 33 A.D.

same time fully God and fully Man. On that, the central tradition of the Church never wavered. It is taken for granted from the beginning by those who have authority to speak.

But a mystery is necessarily, because it is a mystery, incomprehensible; therefore man, being a reasonable being, is perpetually attempting to rationalize it. So it was with this mystery. One set would say Christ was only a man, though a man endowed with special powers. Another set, at the opposite extreme, would say He was a manifestation of the Divine. His human nature was a thing of illusion. They played the changes between those two extremes indefinitely.

Well, the Arian heresy was, as it were, the summing up and conclusion of all these movements on the unorthodox side—that is, of all those movements which did not accept the full mystery of the two natures.

Since it is very difficult to rationalize the union of the Infinite with the finite, since there is an apparent contradiction between the two terms, this final form into which the confusion of heresies settled down was a declaration that Our Lord was as much of the Divine Essence as it was possible for a creature to be, but that He was nonetheless a creature. He was not the Infinite and Omnipotent God who must be of His nature one and indivisible, and could not (so they said) be at the same time a limited human being, moving and having His being in the temporal sphere.

Arianism (I will later describe the origin of the name) was willing to grant Our Lord every kind of honor and majesty short of the full nature of the Godhead. He was created (or, if people did not like the word "created," then He "came forth") from the Godhead before all other effects thereof. Through Him the world was created. He was granted, one might say (paradoxically), all the divine attributes—except divinity.

Essentially this movement sprang from exactly the same source as any other rationalistic movement from the beginning to our own time. It sprang from the desire to visualize clearly and simply something which is beyond the grasp of human vision and comprehension. Therefore, although it began by giving to Our Lord every possible honor and glory short of the actual Godhead, it would inevitably have led in the long run into mere unitarianism and the treating of Our Lord at last as a prophet and, however exalted, no more than a prophet.

As all heresies necessarily breathe the air of the time in which they arise, and are necessarily a reflection of the philosophy of whatever non-Catholic ideas are prevalent at the moment they arise, Arianism spoke in the terms of its day. It did not begin as a similar movement would begin today, by making Our Lord a mere man and nothing else. Still less did it deny the supernatural as a whole. The time in which it arose (the years round about A.D. 300) was a time in which all society took the supernatural for granted. But it spoke of Our Lord as a Supreme Agent of God—a Demiurge—and regarded Him as the first and greatest of those emanations of the Central Godhead through which emanations the fashionable philosophy of the day got over the difficulty of reconciling the Infinite and simple Creator with a complex and finite universe.

So much for the doctrine and for what its rationalistic tendencies would have ended in had it conquered. It would have rendered the new religion something like Mohammedanism or perhaps, seeing the nature of Greek and Roman society, something like an Oriental Calvinism.

At any rate, what I have just set down was the state of this doctrine so long as it flourished: a denial of Our Lord's full Godhead combined with an admission of all His other attributes.

Now when we are talking of the older dead heresies we have to consider the spiritual and therefore social effects of them much more than their mere doctrinal error, although that doctrinal error was the ultimate cause of all their spiritual and social effects. We have to do this because, when a heresy has been long dead, its savor is forgotten. The particular tone and unmistakable impress which it stamped upon society being no longer experienced is non-existent for us, and it has to be resurrected, as it were, by anyone who wants to talk true history. It would be impossible, short of an explanation of this kind, to make a Catholic from Béarn today, a peasant from the neighborhood of Lourdes where Calvinism, once prevalent there, is now dead, understand the savor and individual character of Calvinism as it still survives in Scotland and in sections of the United States. But we must try to realize this now-forgotten Arian atmosphere, because, until we understand its spiritual and therefore social savor, we cannot be said to *know* it really at all.

Further, one must understand this savor or intimate personal character of the movement, and its individual effect on society, in order to understand its importance. There is no greater error in the whole range of bad history than imagining that doctrinal differences, because they are abstract and apparently remote from the practical things of life, are not therefore of intense social effect. Describe to a Chinaman today the doctrinal quarrel of the Reformation, tell him that it was above all a denial of the doctrine of *one* visible church, and a denial of the special authority of its officers. That would be true. He would so far understand what happened at this Reformation as he might understand a mathematical statement. But would that make him understand the French Huguenots of today, the Prussian manner in war and politics, the nature of England and her past since Puritanism arose in this country? Would it make him understand the Orange Lodges or the moral and political systems of, say, Mr. H. G. Wells or Mr. Bernard Shaw? Of course it would not! To give a man the history of tobacco, to give him the chemical formula (if there be such a thing) for nicotine, is not to make him understand what is meant by the smell of tobacco and the effects of smoking it. So it is with Arianism. Merely to say that Arianism was what it was doctrinally is to enunciate a formula, but not to give the thing itself.

When Arianism arose it came upon a society which was already, and had long been, the one Universal Polity of which all civilized men were citizens. There were no separate nations. The Roman Empire was one state from the Euphrates to the Atlantic and from the Sahara to the Scottish Highlands. It was ruled in monarchic fashion by the Commander-in-Chief, or Commanders-in-Chief, of the armies. The title for Commander-in-Chief was "Imperator"—whence we get our word Emperor—and therefore we talk of that State as the "Roman Empire." What the emperor or associated emperors (there had been two of them according to the latest scheme, each with a coadjutor, making four, but these soon coalesced into one supreme head and unique emperor) declared themselves to be, that was the attitude of the empire officially as a whole.

The emperors and therefore the whole official scheme dependent on them had been anti-Christian during the growth of the Catholic Church in the midst of Roman and Greek pagan society. For nearly 300 years they and the official scheme of that society had regarded the increasingly powerful Catholic Church as an alien and very dangerous menace to the traditions and therefore to the strength of the old Greek and Roman pagan world. The Church was, as it were, a state within a state, possessing her own supreme officials, the bishops, and her own organization, which was of a highly developed and powerful kind. She was ubiquitous. She stood in strong contrast with the old world into which she had thrust herself. What would be the life of the one would be the death of the other. The old world defended itself through the action of the last pagan emperors. They launched many persecutions against the Church, ending in one final and very drastic persecution which failed.

The Catholic cause was at first supported by, and at last openly joined by, a man who conquered all other rivals and established himself as supreme monarch over the whole State: the Emperor Constantine the Great ruling from Constantinople, the city which he had founded and called "New Rome." After this the central office of the empire was Christian. By the critical date A.D. 325, not quite three centuries after Pentecost, the Catholic Church had become the official, or at any rate the Palace, Religion of the Empire, and so remained (with one very brief exceptional interval) as long as the empire stood.[3]

---

3. It is not easy to establish the exact point after which the Official Religion of the Roman State, or even of the Emperor, is Christian. Constantine's victory at the Milvian bridge was in the autumn of 312. The Edict of Milan,

But it must not be imagined that the majority of men as yet adhered to the Christian religion, even in the Greek-speaking East. They certainly were not of that religion by anything like a majority in the Latin-speaking West.

As in all great changes throughout history, the parties at issue were minorities inspired with different degrees of enthusiasm or lack of enthusiasm. These minorities had various motives and were struggling each to impose its mental attitude upon the wavering and undecided mass. Of these minorities the Christians were the largest and (what was much more important) the most eager, the most convinced, and the only fully and strictly organized.

The conversion of the Emperor brought over to them large and increasing numbers of the undecided majority. These, perhaps, for the greater part hardly understood the new thing to which they were rallying, and certainly for the most part were not attached to it. But it had finally won politically, and that was enough for them. Many regretted the old gods, but thought it not worthwhile to risk anything in their defense. Very many more cared nothing for what was left of the old gods and not much more for the new Christian fashions. Meanwhile there was a strong minority remaining of highly intelligent and determined pagans. They had on their side not only the traditions of a wealthy governing class, but they had also the great bulk of the best writers and, of course, they also had to strengthen them the recent memories of their long dominance over society.

---

issued by himself and Licinius, which gave toleration to the practice of the Christian Religion throughout the Empire, was issued early in the following year, 313. When Constantine had become sole Emperor he soon lived as a Catechumen of the Christian Church, yet he remained head of the old Pagan religious organization as *Pontifex Maximus.* He was not baptized until the eve of his death, in 337. And though he summoned and presided over gatherings of Christian Bishops, they were still but a separate body in a society mainly Pagan. Constantine's own son and successor had sympathies with the old dying Paganism. The Senate did not change for a lifetime. For active official destruction of the lingering Pagan worship men had to wait till Theodosius at the very end of the century. The whole affair covers one long human life: over eighty years.

There was yet another element of that world, separate from all the rest and one which it is extremely important for us to understand: the Army. Why it is so important for us to understand the position of the Army will be described in a moment.

When the power of Arianism was manifested in those first years of the official Christian Empire and its universal government throughout the Graeco-Roman world, Arianism became the nucleus or center of many forces which would be, of themselves, indifferent to its doctrine. It became the rallying point for many strongly surviving traditions from the older world: traditions not religious, but intellectual, social, moral, literary and all the rest of it.

We might put it vividly enough in modern slang by saying that Arianism, thus vigorously present in the new great discussions within the body of the Christian Church when first that Church achieved official support and became the official religion of the Empire, attracted all the "high-brows," at least half the snobs and nearly all the sincere idealistic tories—the "die hards"—whether nominally Christian or not. It attracted, as we know, great numbers of those who *were* definitely Christian. But it was also the rallying point of these non-Christian forces which were of such great importance in the society of the day.

A great number of the old noble families were reluctant to accept the social revolution implied by the triumph of the Christian Church. They naturally sided with a movement which they instinctively felt to be spiritually opposed to the life and survival of that Church and which carried with it an atmosphere of social superiority over the populace. The Church relied upon and was supported at the end by the masses. Men of old family tradition and wealth found the Arian more sympathetic than the ordinary Catholic and a better ally for gentlemen.

Many intellectuals were in the same position. These had not pride of family and old social traditions from the past, but they had pride of culture. They remembered with regret the former prestige of the pagan philosophers. They thought that this great revolution from paganism to Catholicism would destroy the old cultural traditions and their own cultural position.

The mere snobs, who are always a vast body in any society—that is, the people who have no opinions of their own but who follow what they believe to be the honorific thing of the moment—would be divided. Perhaps the majority of them would follow the official court movement and attach themselves openly to the new religion. But there would always be a certain number who would think it more "*chic*," more "the thing" to profess sympathy with the old pagan traditions, the great old pagan families, the long-inherited venerable pagan culture and literature and all the rest of it. All these reinforced the Arian movement because it was destructive of Catholicism.

Arianism had yet another ally, and the nature of that alliance is so subtle that it requires very careful examination. It had for ally the tendency of government in an absolute monarchy to be half-afraid of emotions present in the minds of the people, and especially in the poorer people: emotions which if they spread and became enthusiastic and captured the mass of the people might become too strong to be ruled and would have to be bowed to. There is here a difficult paradox, but one important to be recognized.

Absolute government, especially in the hands of one man, would seem, on the surface, to be opposed to popular government. The two sound contradictory to those who have not seen absolute monarchy at work. To those who have, it is just the other way. Absolute government is the support of the masses against the power of wealth in the hands of a few, or the power of armies in the hands of a few. Therefore one might imagine that the imperial power of Constantinople would have had sympathy with the popular Catholic masses rather than with the intellectuals and the rest who followed Arianism. But we must remember that while absolute government has for its very cause of existence the defense of the masses against the powerful few, yet it likes to rule. It does not like to feel that there is in the State a rival to its own power. It does not like to feel that great decisions may be imposed by organizations other than its own official organization. That is why even the most Christian emperors and their officials always had at the back of their minds, during the first lifetime of the Arian movement, a *potential* sympathy with Arianism, and that is why this potential sympathy in some cases appears as actual sympathy and as a public declaration of Arianism on their part.

There was yet one more ally to Arianism through which it almost triumphed—the Army.

In order to understand how powerful such an ally was we must appreciate what the Roman Army meant in those days and of what it was composed.

The Army was, of course, in mere numbers, only a small fraction of society. We are not certain what those numbers were; at the most they may have come to half a million—they were probably a good deal less. But to judge by numbers in the matter would be ridiculous. The Army was normally half, or more than half, the State. The Army was the true cement, to use one metaphor, the framework to use another metaphor, the binding force and the support and the very material *self* of the Roman Empire in that fourth century; it had been so for centuries before and was to remain so for further generations.

It is absolutely essential to understand this point, for it explains three-fourths of what happened, not only in the case of the Arian heresy but of everything else between the days of Marius (under whose administration the Roman Army first became professional), and the Mohammedan attack upon Europe, that is, from more than a century before the Christian era to the early seventh century. The social and political position of the Army explains all those seven hundred years and more.

The Roman Empire was a military state. It was not a civilian state. Promotion to power was through the Army. The conception of glory and success, the attainment of wealth in many cases, in nearly all cases the attainment of political power, depended on the Army in those days, just as it depends upon money-lending, speculation, caucuses, manipulation of votes, bosses and newspapers nowadays.

The Army had originally consisted of Roman citizens, all of whom were Italians. Then as the power of the Roman State spread, it took in auxiliary troops, people following local chieftains and affiliated to the Roman military system and even recruited its regular ranks from up and down the empire in every province. There were many Gauls—that is Frenchmen—in the Army, many Spaniards, and so forth, before the first one hundred years of the empire had run out. In the next two hundred years—that is, in the two hundred years A.D. 100-300, leading up to the Arian heresy—the Army had become more and more recruited from what we call "Barbarians," a term which meant not savages but people outside the strict limits of the Roman Empire. They were easier to discipline, they were much cheaper to hire than citizens were. They were also less used to the arts and comforts of civilization than the citizens within the frontiers. Great numbers of them were German, but there were many Slavs and a good many Moors and Arabs and Saracens and not a few Mongols even, drifting in from the East.

This great body of the Roman Army was strictly bound together by its discipline, but still more by its professional pride. It was a long service army. A man belonged to it from his adolescence to his middle age. No one else except the Army had any physical power. There could be no question of resisting it by force, and it was in a sense the government. Its commander-in-chief was the absolute monarch of the whole state. *Now the army went solidly Arian.*

That is the capital mark of the whole affair. But for the Army, Arianism would never have meant what it did. With the Army—and the Army wholeheartedly on its side—Arianism all but triumphed and managed to survive, even when it represented little more than the troops and their chief officers.

It was true that a certain number of German troops from outside the Empire had been converted by Arian missionaries at a moment when high society was Arian. But that was not the main reason that the Army as a whole went Arian. The Army went Arian because it felt Arianism to be the distinctive thing which made it superior to the civilian masses, just as Arianism was a distinctive thing which made the intellectual feel superior to the popular masses. The soldiers, whether of barbaric or civilized recruitment, felt sympathy with Arianism for the same reason that the old pagan families felt sympathy with Arianism. The Army then, and especially the Army chiefs, backed the new heresy for all they were worth, and it became a sort of test of whether you were somebody—a soldier as against the despised civilians—or no. One might say that there had arisen a feud between the Army chiefs on the one hand and the Catholic bishops on the other. Certainly there was a division—an official severance between the Catholic populace in towns, the Catholic peasantry in the country and the almost universally Arian soldier; and the enormous effect of this junction between the new heresy and the Army we shall see at work in all that follows.

Now that we have seen what the spirit of Arianism was and what forces were in its favor, let us see how it got its name.

The movement for denying the full Godhead of Christ and making of Him a Creature took its title from one Areios (in the Latin form Arius), a Greek-speaking African cleric rather older than Constantine, and already famous as a religious force some years before Constantine's victories and first imperial power.

Remember that Arius was only a climax to a long movement. What was the cause of his success? Two things combined. First, the momentum of all that came before him. Second, the sudden release of the Church by Constantine. To this should be added undoubtedly something in Arius' own personality. Men of this kind who become leaders do so because they have some personal momentum from their own past impelling them. They would not so become unless there were something in themselves.

I think we may take it that Arius had the effect he had through a convergence of forces. There was a great deal of ambition in him, such as you will find in all heresiarchs. There was a strong element of rationalism. There was also in him enthusiasm for what he believed to be the truth.

His theory was certainly not his own original discovery, but he made it his own; he identified it with his name. Further, he was moved to a dogged resistance against people whom he thought to be persecuting him. He suffered from much vanity, as do nearly all reformers. On the top of all this a rather thin simplicity, "commonsense," which at once appeals to multitudes. But he would never have had his success but for something eloquent about him and a driving power.

He was already a man of position, probably from the Cyrenaica (now an Italian colony in North Africa east of Tripoli), though he was talked of as being Alexandrian, because it was in Alexandria that he lived. He had been a disciple of the greatest critic of his time, the martyr Lucian of Antioch. In the year 318 he was presiding over the Church of Bucalis in Alexandria, and enjoyed the high favor of the Bishop of the City, Alexander.

Arius went over from Egypt to Caesarea in Palestine, spreading his already well-known set of rationalizing, Unitarian ideas with zeal. Some of the eastern Bishops began to agree with him. It is true that the two main Syrian Bishoprics, Antioch and Jerusalem, stood out; but apparently most of the Syrian hierarchy inclined to listen to Arius.

When Constantine became the master of the whole Empire in 325, Arius appealed to the new master of the world. The great bishop of Alexandria, Alexander, had excommunicated him, but reluctantly. The old heathen Emperor Licinius had protected the new movement.

A battle of vast importance was joined. Men did not know of what importance it was, violently though their emotions were excited. Had this movement for rejecting the full divinity of Our Lord gained the victory, all our civilization would have been other than what it has been from that day to this. We all know what happens when an attempt to simplify and rationalize the mysteries of the Faith succeeds in any society. We have before us the now ending experiment of the Reformation, and the aged but still very vigorous Mohammedan heresy, which may perhaps appear with renewed vigor in the future. Such rationalistic efforts against the creed produce a gradual social degradation following on the loss of that direct link between human nature and God which is provided by the Incarnation. Human dignity is lessened. The authority of Our Lord is weakened. He appears more and more as a man—perhaps a myth. The substance of Christian life is diluted. It wanes. What began as Unitarianism ends as Paganism.

To settle the quarrel by which all Christian society was divided, a council was ordered by the Emperor to meet, in A.D. 325, at the town of Nicaea, fifty miles from the capital, on the Asiatic side of the Straits. The Bishops were summoned to convene there from the whole Empire, even from districts outside the Empire where Christian missionaries had planted the Faith. The great bulk of those who came were from the Eastern Empire, but the West was represented, and, what was of the first importance, delegates arrived from the Primatial See of Rome; but for their adherence the decrees of the Council would not have held. As it was, their presence gave full validity to these Decrees. The reaction against the innovation of Arius was so strong that at this Council of Nicaea he was overwhelmed.

In that first great defeat, when the strong vital tradition of Catholicism had asserted itself and Arius was condemned, the creed which his followers had drawn up was trampled underfoot as a blasphemy, but the spirit behind that creed and behind that revolt was to re-arise.

It re-arose at once, and it can be said that Arianism was actually strengthened by its first superficial defeat. This paradox was due to a cause you will find at work in many forms of conflict. The defeated adversary learns from his first rebuff the character of the thing he has attacked; he discovers its weak points; he learns how his opponent may be confused and into what compromises that opponent may be led. He is therefore better prepared after his check than he was at the first onslaught. So it was with Arianism.

In order to understand the situation we must appreciate the

point that Arianism, founded like all heresies on an error in doctrine—that is, on something which can be expressed in a dead formula of mere words—soon began to live, like all heresies at their beginning, with a vigorous new life and character and savor of its own. The quarrel which filled the third century from 325 onwards for a lifetime was not after its first years a quarrel between opposing forms of words, the difference between which may appear slight; it became very early in the struggle a quarrel between opposing spirits and characters: a quarrel between two opposing *personalities,* such as human personalities are: on the one side the Catholic temper and tradition, on the other a soured, proud temper, which would have destroyed the Faith.

Arianism learned from its first heavy defeat at Nicaea to compromise on forms, on the wording of doctrine, so that it might preserve and spread, with less opposition, its heretical spirit. The first conflict had turned on the use of a Greek word which means "of the same substance with." The Catholics, affirming the full Godhead of Our Lord, insisted on the use of this word, which implied that the Son was of the same Divine substance as the Father; that He was of the same Being: *i.e.,* Godship. It was thought sufficient to present this word as a test. The Arians—it was thought—would always refuse to accept the word and could thus be distinguished from the Orthodox and rejected.

But many Arians were prepared to compromise by accepting the mere word and denying the spirit in which it should be read. They were willing to admit that Christ was of the Divine essence, but not fully God; not uncreated. When the Arians began this new policy of verbal compromise, the Emperor Constantine and his successors regarded that policy as an honest opportunity for reconciliation and reunion. The refusal of the Catholics to be deceived became, in the eyes of those who thought thus, mere obstinancy; and in the eyes of the Emperor, factious rebellion and inexcusable disobedience. "Here are you people, who call yourself the only real Catholics, prolonging and needlessly embittering a mere faction-fight. Because you have the popular names behind you, you feel yourselves the masters of your fellows. Such arrogance is intolerable.

"The other side have accepted your main point; why cannot you now settle the quarrel and come together again? By holding out you split society into two camps; you disturb the peace of the Empire, and are as criminal as you are fanatical."

That is what the official world tended to put forward and honestly believed.

The Catholics answered: "The heretics have *not* accepted our main point. They have subscribed to an Orthodox phrase, but they interpret that phrase in an heretical fashion. They will repeat that Our Lord is of Divine nature, but *not* that He is fully God, for they still say He was created. Therefore we will not allow them to enter our communion. To do so would be to endanger the vital principle by which the Church exists, the principle of the Incarnation, and the Church is essential to the Empire and Mankind."

At this point, there entered the battle that personal force which ultimately won the victory for Catholicism: St. Athanasius. It was the tenacity and single aim of St. Athanasius, Patriarch of Alexandria, the great Metropolitan See of Egypt, which decided the issue. He enjoyed a position of advantage, for Alexandria was the second most important town in the Eastern Empire and, as a Bishopric, one of the first four in the world. He further enjoyed popular backing, which never failed him, and which made his enemies hesitate to take extreme measures against him. But all this would not have sufficed had not the man himself been what he was.

At the time when he sat at the Council of Nicaea in 325 he was still a young man—probably not quite thirty; and he only sat there as Deacon, although already his strength and eloquence were remarkable. He lived to be seventy-six or seventy-seven years of age, dying in A.D. 373, and during nearly the whole of that long life he maintained with inflexible energy the full Catholic doctrine of the Trinity.

When the first compromise with Arianism was suggested, Athanasius was already Archbishop of Alexandria. Constantine ordered him to re-admit Arius to Communion. He refused.

It was a step most perilous, because all men admitted the full power of the Monarch over Life and Death, and regarded rebellion as the worst of crimes. Athanasius was also felt to be outrageous and extravagant, because opinion in the official world, among men of social influence, and throughout the Army, upon which everything then reposed, was strong that the compromise ought to be accepted. Athanasius was exiled to Gaul, but Athanasius in exile was even more formidable than Athanasius in Alexandria. His presence in the West had the effect of reinforcing the strong Catholic feeling of all that part of the Empire.

He was recalled. The sons of Constantine, who succeeded one after the other to the Empire, vacillated between the policy of securing popular support—which was Catholic—and of securing the support of the Army—which was Arian. Most of all did the Court lean towards Arianism because it disliked the growing power of the organized Catholic Clergy, rival to the lay power of the State. The last and longest-lived of Constantine's sons and successors, Constantius, became very definitely Arian. Athanasius was exiled over and over again, but the Cause of which he was champion was growing in strength.

When Constantius died in 361, he was succeeded by a nephew of Constantine's, Julian the Apostate. This Emperor went over to the large surviving Pagan body and came near to re-establishing Paganism; for the power of an individual Emperor was in that day overwhelming. But he was killed in battle against the Persians—and his successor, Jovian, was definitely Catholic.

However, the see-saw still went on. In 367, St. Athanasius, being then an old man of at least seventy years of age, the Emperor Valens exiled him for the fifth time. Finding that the Catholic forces were now too strong, he later recalled him. By this time Athanasius had won his battle. He died as the greatest man of the Roman world. Of such value are sincerity and tenacity, combined with genius.

But the Army remained Arian, and what we have to follow in the generations is the lingering death of Arianism in the Latin-speaking Western part of the Empire; lingering because it was supported by the Chief Generals in command of the Western districts, but doomed because the people as a whole had abandoned it. How it thus died out I shall now describe.

* * *

It is often said that all heresies die. This may be true in the very long run, but it is not necessarily true within any given period of time. It is not even true that the vital principle of a heresy necessarily loses strength with time. The fate of the various heresies has been most various; and the greatest of them, Mohammedanism, is not only still vigorous but is more vigorous over the districts which it originally occupied than is its Christian rival, and much more vigorous and much more co-extensive with its own society than is the Catholic Church with our Western civilization which is the product of Catholicism.

Arianism, however, was one of those heresies which *did* die. The same fate has overtaken Calvinism in our own day. This does not mean that the general moral effect or atmosphere of the heresy disappears from among men, but that its creative doctrines are no longer believed in, so that its vitality is lost and must ultimately disappear.

Geneva today, for instance, is morally a Calvinist city, although it has a Catholic minority sometimes very nearly equal to half its total numbers, sometimes actually becoming (I believe) a slight majority. But there is not one man of a hundred in Geneva today who accepts Calvin's highly defined theology. The doctrine is dead; its effects on society survive.

Arianism died in two fashions, corresponding to the two halves into which the Roman Empire—which was in those days, for its citizens, the whole civilized world—fell.

The Eastern half had Greek for its official language and it was governed from Constantinople, which was also called Byzantium.

It included Egypt, North Africa as far as Cyrene, the East Coast of the Adriatic, the Balkans, Asia Minor, Syria as far (roughly) as the Euphrates. It was in this part of the Empire that Arianism had sprung up and proved so powerful that between A.D. 300 and A.D. 400 it very nearly conquered.

The Imperial Court had wavered between Arianism and Catholicism with one momentary lapse back into paganism. But before the century was over, that is well before the year A.D. 400, the Court was definitely Catholic and seemed certain to remain so. As I explained above, although the Emperor and his surrounding officials (which I have called "the Court") were theoretically all-powerful (for the constitution was an absolute monarchy and men could not think in any other terms in those days), yet, at least as powerful, and less subject to change, was the army on which the whole of that society reposed. And the army meant the generals; the generals of the army were for the most part, and permanently, Arian.

When the central power, the Emperor and his officials, had become permanently Catholic the spirit of the military was still in the main Arian, and that is why the underlying ideas of Arianism—that is, the doubt whether Our Lord was or could be really God—survived after formal Arianism had ceased to be preached and accepted among the populace.

On this account, because the spirit which had underlain Arianism (the doubt on the full divinity of Christ) went on, there arose a number of what may be called "derivatives" from Arianism, or "secondary forms" of Arianism.

Men continued to suggest that there was only one nature in Christ, the end of which suggestion would necessarily have been a popular idea that Christ was only a man. When that failed to capture the official machine, though it continued to affect millions of people, there was another suggestion made that there was only one Will in Christ, not a human will and a divine will, but a single will.

Before these there had been a revival of the old idea, previous to Arianism and upheld by early heretics in Syria, that the divinity only came into Our Lord during His lifetime. He was born no more than a man, and Our Lady was the mother of no more than a man—and so on. In all their various forms and under all their technical names (Monophysites, Monothelites, Nestorians, the names of the principal three—and there were any number of others) these movements throughout the Eastern or Greek half of the Empire were efforts at escaping from, or rationalizing, the full mystery of the Incarnation; and their survival depended on the jealousy felt by the army for the civilian society round it, and on the lingering remains of pagan hostility to the Christian mysteries as a whole. Of course they depended also on the eternal human tendency to rationalize and to reject what is beyond the reach of reason.

But there was another factor in the survival of the secondary effects of Arianism in the East. It was the factor which is called today in European politics "Particularism," that is, the tendency of a part of the state to separate itself from the rest and to live its own life. When this feeling becomes so strong that men are willing to suffer and die for it, it takes the form of a Nationalist revolution. An example of such was the feeling of the southern Slavs against the Austrian Empire, which feeling give rise to the Great War. Now this discontent of provinces and districts with the Central Power by which they had been governed increased as time went on in the Eastern Empire; and a convenient way of expressing it was to favor any kind of criticism against the official religion of the Empire. That is why great bodies in the East (and notably a large proportion of the people in the Egyptian province) favored the Monophysite heresy. It expressed their dissatisfaction with the despotic rule of Constantinople and with the taxes imposed upon them and with the promotion given to those near the Court at the expense of the provincials—and all the rest of their grievances.

Thus the various derivatives from Arianism survived in the Greek Eastern half of the Empire, although the official world had long gone back to Catholicism. This also explains why you find all over the East today large numbers of schismatic Christians, mainly Monophysite, sometimes Nestorian, sometimes of lesser communities, whom not all these centuries of Mohammedan oppression have been able to unite with the main Christian body.

What put an end, not to these sects, for they still exist, but to their *importance,* was the sudden rise of that enormous force, antagonistic to the whole Greek world—Islam: the new Mohammedan heresy out of the desert, which rapidly became a counter-religion; the implacable enemy of all the older Christian bodies. The death of Arianism in the East was the swamping of the mass of the Christian Eastern Empire by Arabian conquerors. In the face of that disaster the Christians who remained independent reacted towards orthodoxy as their one chance of survival, and that is how even the secondary effects of Arianism died out in the countries free from subjugation to the Mohammedans in the East.

In the West the fortunes of Arianism are quite different. In the West Arianism died altogether. It ceased to be. It left no derivatives to carry on a lingering life.

The story of this death of Arianism in the West is commonly misunderstood because most of our history has been written hitherto on a misconception of what European Christian society was like in Western Europe during the fourth, fifth and sixth centuries, that is, between the time when Constantine left Rome and set up the new capital of the Empire, Byzantium, and the date when, in the early seventh century (from A.D. 633 onwards), the Mohammedan invasion burst upon the world.

What we are commonly told is that the Western Empire was overrun by savage tribes called "Goths" and "Visigoths" and "Vandals" and "Suevi" and "Franks" who "conquered" the Western Roman Empire—that is, Britain and Gaul and the civilized part of Germany on the Rhine and the upper Danube, Italy, North Africa and Spain.

The official language of all this part was the Latin language. The Mass was said in Latin, whereas in most of the Eastern Empire it was said in Greek. The laws were in Latin, and all the acts of administration were in Latin. There was no barbarian conquest, but there was a continuation of what had been going on for centuries, an infiltration of people from outside the Empire into the Empire because within the Empire they could get the advantages of civilization. There was also the fact that the army on which everything depended was at last almost entirely recruited from the barbarians. As society gradually got old and it was found difficult to administer distant places, to gather the taxes from far away into the central treasury, or to impose an edict over remote regions, the government of those regions tended to be taken over more and more by the leading officers of the barbarian tribes, who were now Roman soldiers; that is, their chieftains and leaders.

In this way were formed local governments in France and Spain and even Italy itself which, while they still felt themselves to be part of the Empire, were practically independent.

For instance, when it became difficult to govern Italy from so far off as Constantinople, the Emperor sent a general to govern in his place and when this general became too strong he sent another general to supersede him. This second general (Theodoric) was also, like all the others, a barbarian chief by birth, though he was the son of one who had been taken into the Roman service and had himself been brought up at the Court of the Emperor.

This second general became in his turn practically independent.

The same thing happened in southern France and in Spain. The local generals took over power. They were barbarian chiefs who handed over this power, that is, the nominating to official posts and the collecting of taxes, to their descendants.

Then there was the case of North Africa—what we call today Morocco, Algiers and Tunis. Here the quarrelling factions, all of which were disconnected with direct government from Byzantium, called in a group of Slav soldiers who had migrated into the Roman Empire and had been taken over as a military force. They were called the Vandals; and they took over the government of the province which worked from Carthage.

Now all these local governments of the West (the Frankish general and his group of soldiers in northern France, the Visigothic one in southern France and Spain, the Burgundian one in southeastern France, the other Gothic one in Italy, the Vandal one in North Africa) were at issue with the official government of the Empire on the point of religion. The Frankish one in northeastern France and what we call today, Belgium, was still pagan. All the others were Arian.

I have explained above what this meant. It was not so much a doctrinal feeling as a social one. The Gothic general and the Vandal general who were chiefs over their own soldiers felt it was grander to be Arians than to be Catholics like the mass of the populace. They were the army; and the army was too grand to accept the general popular religion. It was a feeling very much like that which you may see surviving in Ireland still, in places, and which was universal there until quite lately: a feeling that "ascendency" went properly with anti-Catholicism.

Since there is no stronger force in politics than this force of social superiority, it took a very long time for the little local courts to drop their Arianism. I call them little because, although they collected taxes from very wide areas, it was merely as administrators. Their actual numbers were small compared with the mass of the Catholic population.

While the governors and their courts in Italy and Spain and Gaul and Africa still clung with pride to their ancient Arian name and character, two things, one sudden, the other gradual, militated against both their local power and their Arianism.

The first, sudden thing was the fact that the general of the Franks who had ruled in Belgium conquered with his very small force another local general in northern France—a man who governed a district lying to the west of him. Both armies were absurdly small, each of about 4,000 men; and it is a very good example of what the times were like that the beaten army, after the battle, at once joined the victors. It also shows what times were like that it seemed perfectly natural for a Roman general commanding no more than 4,000 men to begin with, and only 8,000 men after the first success, to take over the administration—taxes, courts of law and all the imperial forms—over a very wide district. He took over the great mass of northern France just as his colleagues, with similar forces, took over official action in Spain and Italy and elsewhere.

Now it so happened that this Frankish general (whose real name we hardly know, because it has come down to us in various distorted forms, but best known as "Clovis") was a pagan: something exceptional and even scandalous in the military forces of the day when nearly all important people had become Christians.

But this scandal proved a blessing in disguise to the Church, for the man Clovis being a pagan and never having been Arian, it was possible to convert him directly to Catholicism, the popular religion; and when he had accepted Catholicism he at once had behind him the whole force of the millions of citizens and the organized priesthood and Bishoprics of the Church. He was the one popular general; all the others were at issue with their subjects. He found it easy to levy great bodies of armed men because he had popular feeling with him. He took over the government of the Arian generals in the South, easily defeating them, and his levies became the biggest of the military forces in the Western Latin-speaking Empire. He was not strong enough to take over Italy and Spain, still less Africa, but he shifted the center of gravity away from the decaying Arian tradition of the Roman army—now no more than small dwindling groups.

So much for the sudden blow which was struck against Arianism in the West. The gradual process which hastened the decay of Arianism was of a different kind. With every year that passed, it was becoming, in the decay of society, more and more difficult to collect taxes, to keep up a revenue, and therefore to repair roads and harbors and public buildings and keep order and do all the rest of public work.

With this financial decay of government and the social disintegration accompanying it, the little groups who were nominally the local governments lost their prestige. In, say, the year 450 it was a fine thing to be an Arian in Paris or Toledo or Carthage or Arles or Toulouse or Ravenna; but 100 years later, by say, 550, the social prestige of Arianism had gone. It paid everybody who wanted to "get on" to be a Catholic; and the dwindling little official Arian groups were despised even when they acted savagely in their disappointment, as they did in Africa. They lost ground.

The consequence was that after a certain delay, all the Arian governments in the West either became Catholic (as in the case of Spain) or, as happened in much of Italy and the whole of North Africa, they were taken over again by the direct rule of the Roman Empire from Byzantium.

This last experiment did not continue long. There was another body of barbarian soldiers, still Arian, who came in from the northeastern provinces and took over the government in northern and central Italy and shortly afterwards the Mohammedan invasion swept over North Africa and ultimately over Spain and even penetrated into Gaul. Direct Roman administration, so far from surviving Western Europe, died out. Its last effective existence in the South was swamped by Islam. But long before this happened, Arianism in the West was dead.

This is the fashion in which the first of the great heresies which threatened at one moment to undermine and destroy the whole of Catholic society disappeared. The process had taken almost 300 years, and it is interesting to note that so far as doctrines are concerned, about that space of time, or a little more, sufficed to take the substance out of the various main heresies of the Protestant Reformers.

They, too, had almost triumphed in the middle of the sixteenth century, when Calvin, their chief figure, all but upset the French Monarchy. They also had wholly lost their vitality by the middle of the nineteenth—300 years.

4

THE GREAT AND ENDURING HERESY
OF MOHAMMED

It might have appeared to any man watching affairs in the earlier years of the seventh century—say from 600 to 630—that the only one great main assault having been made against the Church, Arianism and its derivatives, that assault having been repelled and the Faith having won its victory, it was now secure for an indefinite time.

Christendom would have to fight for its life, of course, against outward unchristian things, that is, against Paganism. The nature worshippers of the high Persian civilization to the east would attack us in arms and try to overwhelm us. The savage paganism of barbaric tribes, the Scandinavian, German, Slav and Mongol, in the north and center of Europe would also attack Christendom and try to destroy it. The populations subject to Byzantium would continue to parade heretical views as a label for their grievances. But the main effort of heresy, at least, had failed—so it seemed. Its object, the undoing of a united Catholic civilization, had been missed. The rise of no major heresy need henceforth be feared, still less the consequent disruption of Christendom.

By A.D. 630 all Gaul had long been Catholic. The last of the Arian generals and their garrisons in Italy and Spain had become orthodox. The Arian generals and garrisons of Northern Africa had been conquered by the orthodox armies of the Emperor.

It was just at this moment, a moment of apparently universal and permanent Catholicism, that there fell an unexpected blow of overwhelming magnitude and force. Islam arose—quite suddenly. It came out of the desert and overwhelmed half our civilization.

Islam—the teaching of Mohammed—conquered immediately in arms. Mohammed's Arabian converts charged into Syria and won there two great battles, the first upon the Yarmuk to the east of Palestine in the highlands above the Jordan, the second in Mesopotamia. They went on to overrun Egypt; they pushed further and further into the heart of our Christian civilization with all its grandeur of Rome. They established themselves all over Northern Africa; they raided into Asia Minor, though they did not establish themselves there as yet. They could even occasionally threaten Constantinople itself. At last, a long lifetime after their first victories in Syria, they crossed the Straits of Gibraltar into Western Europe and began to flood Spain. They even got as far as the very heart of Northern France between Poitiers and Tours, less than a hundred years after their first victories in Syria—in A.D. 732.

They were ultimately thrust back to the Pyrenees, but they continued to hold all Spain except the mountainous northwestern corner. They held all Roman Africa, including Egypt, and all Syria. They dominated the whole Mediterranean west and east: held its islands, raided and left armed settlements even on the shores of Gaul and Italy. They spread mightily throughout Hither Asia, overwhelming the Persian realm. They were an increasing menace to Constantinople. Within a hundred years, a main part of the Roman world had fallen under the power of this new and strange force from the Desert.

Such a revolution had never been. No earlier attack had been so sudden, so violent or so permanently successful. Within a score of years from the first assault in 634 the Christian Levant had gone: Syria, the cradle of the Faith, and Egypt with Alexandria, the mighty Christian See. Within a lifetime half the wealth and nearly half the territory of the Christian Roman Empire was in the hands of Mohammedan masters and officials, and the mass of the population was becoming affected more and more by this new thing.

Mohammedan government and influence had taken the place of Christian government and influence, and were on the way to making the bulk of the Mediterranean on the east and the south Mohammedan.

We are about to follow the fortunes of this extraordinary thing which still calls itself Islam, that is, "The Acceptation" of the morals and simple doctrines which Mohammed had preached.

I shall later describe the historical origin of the thing, giving the dates of its progress and the stages of its original success. I shall describe the consolidation of it, its increasing power and the threat which it remained to our civilization. It very nearly destroyed us. It kept up the battle against Christendom actively for a thousand years, and the story is by no means over; the power of Islam may at any moment re-arise.

But before following that story we must grasp the two fundamental things—*first,* the nature of Mohammedanism, *second,* the essential cause of its sudden and, as it were, miraculous success over so many thousands of miles of territory and so many millions of human beings.

Mohammedanism was a *heresy:* that is the essential point to grasp before going any further. It began as a heresy, not as a new religion. It was not a pagan contrast with the Church; it was not an alien enemy. It was a perversion of Christian doctrine. Its vitality and endurance soon gave it the appearance of a new religion, but those who were contemporary with its rise saw it for what it was—not a denial, but an adaptation and a misuse, of the Christian thing. It differed from most (not from all) heresies in this, that it did not arise within the bounds of the Christian Church. The chief heresiarch, Mohammed himself, was not, like most heresiarchs, a man of Catholic birth and doctrine to begin with. He sprang from pagans. But that which he taught was in the main Catholic doctrine, oversimplified. It was the great Catholic world—on the frontiers of which he lived, whose influence was all around him and whose territories he had known by travel—which inspired his convictions. He came of, and mixed with, the degraded idolaters of the Arabian wilderness, the conquest of which had never seemed worth the Romans' while.

He took over very few of those old pagan ideas which might have been native to him from his descent. On the contrary, he preached and insisted upon a whole group of ideas which were peculiar to the Catholic Church and distinguished it from the paganism which it had conquered in the Greek and Roman civilization. Thus the very foundation of his teaching was that prime Catholic doctrine, the unity and omnipotence of God. The attributes of God he also took over in the main from Catholic doctrine: the personal nature, the all-goodness, the timelessness, the providence of God, His creative power as the origin of all things, and His sustenance of all things by His power alone. The world of good spirits and angels and of evil spirits in rebellion against God was part of the teaching, with a chief evil spirit, such as Christendom had recognized. Mohammed preached with insistence that prime Catholic doctrine, on the human side—the immortality of the soul and its responsibility for actions in this life, coupled with the consequent doctrine of punishment and reward after death.

If anyone sets down those points that orthodox Catholicism has in common with Mohammedanism, and those points only, one might imagine if one went no further that there should have been no cause of quarrel. Mohammed would almost seem in this aspect to be a sort of missionary, preaching and spreading by the energy of his character the chief and fundamental doctrines of the Catholic Church among those who had hitherto been degraded pagans of the Desert. He gave to Our Lord the highest reverence, and to Our Lady also, for that matter. On the day of judgment (another Catholic idea which he taught) it was Our Lord, according to Mohammed, who would be the judge of mankind, not he, Mohammed. The Mother of Christ, Our Lady, "the Lady Miriam" was ever for him the first of womankind. His followers even got from the early fathers some vague hint of her Immaculate Conception.[4]

---

4. It was from this fact that certain French writers opposed to the Church got their enormous blunder, that the Immaculate Conception came to us

But the central point where this new heresy struck home with a mortal blow against Catholic tradition was a full denial of the Incarnation.

Mohammed did not merely take the first steps toward that denial, as the Arians and their followers had done; he advanced a clear affirmation, full and complete, against the whole doctrine of an incarnate God. He taught that Our Lord was the greatest of all the prophets, but still only a prophet: a man like other men. He eliminated the Trinity altogether.

With that denial of the Incarnation went the whole sacramental structure. He refused to know anything of the Eucharist, with its Real Presence; he stopped the sacrifice of Mass, and therefore the institution of a special priesthood. In other words, he, like so many other lesser heresiarchs, founded his heresy on simplification.

Catholic doctrine was true (he seemed to say), but it had become encumbered with false accretions; it had become complicated by needless man-made additions, including the idea that its founder was Divine, and the growth of a parasitical caste of priests who battened on a late, imagined, system of Sacraments which they alone could administer. All those corrupt accretions must be swept away.

There is thus a very great deal in common between the enthusiasm with which Mohammed's teaching attacked the priesthood, the Mass and the Sacraments, and the enthusiasm with which Calvinism, the central motive force of the Reformation, did the same. As we all know, the new teaching relaxed the marriage laws—but in practice this did not affect the mass of his followers who still remained monogamous. It made divorce as easy as possible, for the sacramental idea of marriage disappeared. It insisted upon the equality of men, and it necessarily had that further factor in which it resembled Calvinism— the sense of predestination, the sense of fate; of what the fol-

---

from Mohammedan sources! Gibbon, of course, copied his masters blindly here—as he always does, and he repeats the absurdity in his *Decline and Fall*.

lowers of John Knox were always calling "the immutable decrees of God."

Mohammed's teaching never developed among the mass of his followers, or in his own mind, a detailed theology. He was content to accept all that appealed to him in the Catholic scheme and to reject all that seemed to him, and to so many others of his time, too complicated or mysterious to be true. Simplicity was the note of the whole affair; and since all heresies draw their strength from some true doctrine, Mohammedanism drew its strength from the true Catholic doctrines which it retained: the equality of men before God—"All true believers are brothers." It zealously preached and throve on the paramount claims of justice, social and economic.

Now, why did this new, simple, energetic heresy have its sudden overwhelming success?

One answer is that it won battles. It won them at once, and thoroughly, as we shall see when we come to the history of the thing. But winning battles would not have made Islam permanent or even strong had there not been a state of affairs awaiting some such message and ready to accept it.

Both in the world of Hither Asia and in the Graeco-Roman world of the Mediterranean, but especially in the latter, society had fallen, much as our society has today, into a tangle wherein the bulk of men were disappointed and angry and seeking for a solution to the whole group of social strains. There was indebtedness everywhere; the power of money and consequent usury. There was slavery everywhere. Society reposed upon it, as ours reposes upon wage slavery today. There was weariness and discontent with theological debate, which, for all its intensity, had grown out of touch with the masses. There lay upon the freemen, already tortured with debt, a heavy burden of imperial taxation; and there was the irritant of existing central government interfering with men's lives; there was the tyranny of the lawyers and their charges.

To all this, Islam came as a vast relief and a solution of strain. The slave who admitted that Mohammed was the prophet of God and that the new teaching had, therefore, divine authority, ceased to be a slave. The slave who adopted Islam was henceforward free. The debtor who "accepted" was rid of his debts. Usury was forbidden. The small farmer was relieved not only of his debts but of his crushing taxation. Above all, justice could be had without buying it from lawyers...All this in theory. The practice was not nearly so complete. Many a convert remained a debtor, many were still slaves. But wherever Islam conquered, there was a new spirit of freedom and relaxation.

It was the combination of all these things, the attractive simplicity of the doctrine, the sweeping away of clerical and imperial discipline, the huge immediate practical advantage of freedom for the slave and riddance of anxiety for the debtor, the crowning advantage of free justice under few and simple new laws easily understood—that formed the driving force behind the astonishing Mohammedan social victory. The courts were everywhere accessible to all without payment and giving verdicts which all could understand. The Mohammedan movement was essentially a "Reformation," and we can discover numerous affinities between Islam and the Protestant Reformers—on Images, on the Mass, on Celibacy, etc.

The marvel seems to be, not so much that the new emancipation swept over men much as we might imagine Communism to sweep over our industrial world today, but that there should still have remained, as there remained for generations, a prolonged and stubborn resistance to Mohammedanism.

There you have, I think, the nature of Islam and of its first original blaze of victory.

We have just seen what was the main cause of Islam's extraordinarily rapid spread; a complicated and fatigued society, and one burdened with the institution of slavery; one, moreover, in which millions of peasants in Egypt, Syria and all the East, crushed with usury and heavy taxation, were offered immediate relief by the new creed, or rather, the new heresy. Its note was simplicity and therefore it was suited to the popular mind in a society where hitherto a restricted class had pursued its quarrels on theology and government.

That is the main fact which accounts for the sudden spread of Islam after its first armed victory over the armies rather than the people of the Greek-speaking Eastern empire. But this alone would not account for two other equally striking triumphs. The first was the power the new heresy showed of absorbing the Asiatic people of the Near East, Mesopotamia and the mountain land between it and India. The second was the wealth and splendor of the Caliphate (that is, of the central Mohammedan monarchy) in the generations coming immediately after the first sweep of victory.

The first of these points, the spread over Mesopotamia and Persia and the mountain land towards India, was not, as in the case of the sudden successes in Syria and Egypt, due to the appeal of simplicity, freedom from slavery and relief from debt. It was due to a certain underlying historical character in the Near East which has always influenced its society and continues to influence it today. That character is a sort of natural uniformity. There has been inherent in it from times earlier than any known historical record, a sort of instinct for obedience to one religious head, which is also the civil head, and a general similarity of social culture. When we talk of the age-long struggle between Asia and the West, we mean by the word "Asia" all that sparse population of the mountain land beyond Mesopotamia towards India, its permanent influence upon the Mesopotamian plains themselves, and its potential influence upon even the highlands and seacoast of Syria and Palestine.

The struggle between Asia and Europe swings over a vast period like a tide ebbing and flowing. For nearly a thousand years, from the conquest of Alexander to the coming of the Mohammedan Reformers (333 B.C.-A.D. 634), the tide had set eastward; that is, western influences—Greek, and then Greek and Roman—had flooded the debatable land. For a short period of about two and a half to three centuries even Mesopotamia was superficially Greek—in its governing class, at any rate. Then Asia began to flood back again westward. The old Pagan Roman Empire and the Christian Empire, which succeeded it and which was governed from Constantinople, were never able to hold permanently the land beyond the Euphrates. The new push from Asia westward was led by the Persians, and the Persians and Parthians (which last were a division of the Persians) not only kept their hold on Mesopotamia but were able to carry out raids into Roman territory itself, right up to the end of that period. In the last few years before the appearance of Mohammedanism they had appeared on the Mediterranean coast and had sacked Jerusalem.

Now when Islam came with its first furious victorious cavalry charges springing from the desert, it powerfully reinforced this tendency of Asia to reassert itself. The uniformity of temper which is the mark of Asiatic society, responded at once to this new idea of one very simple, personal form of government, sanctified by religion, and ruling with a power theoretically absolute from one center. The Caliphate once established at Baghdad, Baghdad became just what Babylon had been; the central capital of one vast society, giving its tone to all the lands from the Indian borders to Egypt and beyond.

But even more remarkable than the flooding of all near Asia with Mohammedanism in one lifetime was the wealth and splendor and culture of the new Islamic Empire. Islam was in those early centuries (most of the seventh, all the eighth and ninth), the highest material civilization of our occidental world. The city of Constantinople was also very wealthy and enjoyed a very high civilization, which radiated over dependent provinces, Greece and the seaboard of the Aegean and the uplands of Asia Minor, but it was focused in the imperial city; in the greater part of the countrysides, culture was on the decline. In the West it was notoriously so. Gaul and Britain, and in some degree Italy, and the valley of the Danube, fell back towards barbarism. They never became completely barbaric, not even Britain, which was the most remote; but they were harried and impoverished, and lacked proper government. From the fifth century to the early eleventh (say A.D. 450 to A.D. 1030) ran the period which we call "The Dark Ages" of Europe—in spite of Charlemagne's experiment.

So much for the Christian world of that time, against which Islam was beginning to press so heavily; which had lost to Islam the whole of Spain and certain islands and coasts of the central Mediterranean as well. Christendom was under seige from Islam. Islam stood up against us in dominating splendor and wealth and power, and, what was even more important, with superior knowledge in the practical and applied sciences.

Islam preserved the Greek philosophers, the Greek mathematicians and their works, the physical science of the Greek and Roman earlier writers. Islam was also far more lettered than was Christendom. In the mass of the West most men had become illiterate. Even in Constantinople, reading and writing were not as common as they were in the world governed by the Caliph.

One might sum up and say that the contrast between the Mohammedan world of those early centuries and the Christian world which it threatened to overwhelm was like the contrast between a modern industrialized state and a backward, half-developed state next door to it: the contrast between modern Germany, for instance, and its Russian neighbor. The contrast was not as great as that, but the modern parallel helps one to understand it. For centuries to come Islam was to remain a menace, even though Spain was reconquered. In the East it became more than a menace, and spread continually for seven hundred years, until it had mastered the Balkans and the Hungarian plain, and all but occupied Western Europe itself. Islam was the one heresy that nearly destroyed Christendom through its early material and intellectual superiority.

Now why was this? It seems inexplicable when we remember the uncertain and petty personal leaderships, the continual changes of local dynasties, the shifting foundation of the Mohammedan effort. That effort began with the attack of a very few thousand desert horsemen, who were as much drawn by desire for loot as by their enthusiasm for their new doctrines. Those doctrines had been preached to a very sparse body of nomads, boasting but very few permanently inhabited centers. They had originated in a man remarkable indeed for the intensity of his nature, probably more than half convinced, probably also a little mad, and one who had never shown constructive ability—yet Islam conquered.

Mohammed was a camel driver, who had had the good luck to make a wealthy marriage with a woman older than himself. From the security of that position he worked out his visions and enthusiasms, and undertook his propaganda. But it was all done in an ignorant and very small way. There was no organization, and the moment the first bands had succeeded in battle, the leaders began fighting among themselves: not only fighting, but murdering. The story of all the first lifetime, and a little more, after the original rush—the story of the Mohammedan government (such as it was) so long as it was centered in Damascus, is a story of successive intrigue and murder. Yet when the second dynasty which presided for so long over Islam, the Abbasides, with their capital further east at Baghdad, on the Euphrates, restored the old Mesopotamian domination over Syria, ruling also Egypt and all the Mohammedan world, that splendor and science, material power and wealth of which I spoke, arose and dazzled all contemporaries, and we must ask the question again: why was this?

The answer lies in the very nature of the Mohammedan conquest. It did *not,* as has been so frequently repeated, destroy at once what it came across; it did *not* exterminate all those who would not accept Islam. It was just the other way. It was remarkable among the powers which have ruled these lands throughout history for what has wrongly been called its "tolerance." The Mohammedan temper was not tolerant. It was, on the contrary, fanatical and bloodthirsty. It felt no respect for, nor even curiosity about, those from whom it differed. It was absurdly vain of itself, regarding with contempt the high Christian culture about it. It still so regards it even today.

But the conquerors, and those whom they converted and attached to themselves from the native populations, were still too few to govern by force. And (what is more important) they had no idea of organization. They were always slipshod and haphazard. Therefore a very large majority of the conquered remained in their old habits of life and of religion.

Slowly the influence of Islam spread through these, but during the first centuries the great majority in Syria, and even in Mesopotamia and Egypt, were Christian, keeping the Christian Mass, the Christian Gospels, and all the Christian tradition. It was they who preserved the Graeco-Roman civilization from which they descended, and it was that civilization, surviving under the surface of Mohammedan government, which gave their learning and material power to the wide territories which we must call, even so early, "the Mohammedan world," though the bulk of it was not yet Mohammedan in creed.

But there was another—and it is the most important cause. The fiscal cause: the overwhelming wealth of the early Mohammedan Caliphate. The merchant and the tiller of the land, the owner of property and the negotiator, were everywhere relieved by the Mohammedan conquest; for a mass of usury was swept away, as was an intricate system of taxation which had become clogged, ruining the taxpayer without corresponding results for the government. What the Arabian conquerors and their successors in Mesopotamia did was to replace all that by a simple, straight system of tribute.

Whatever was not Mohammedan in the immense Mohammedan Empire—that is, much the most of its population—was subject to a special tribute; and it was this tribute which furnished directly, without loss from the intricacies of bureaucracy, the wealth of the central power; the revenue of the Caliph. That revenue remained enormous during all the first generations. The result was that which always follows upon a high concentration of wealth in one governing center; the whole of the society governed from that center reflects the opulence of its directors.

There we have the explanation of that strange, that unique phenomenon in history—a revolt against civilization which did not destroy civilization; a consuming heresy which did not destroy the Christian religion against which it was directed.

The world of Islam became, and long remained, the heir of the old Graeco-Roman culture and the preserver thereof. Thence

was it that, alone of all the great heresies, Mohammedanism
not only survived, and is, after nearly fourteen centuries, as
strong as ever spiritually. In time it struck roots and established
a civilization of its own over against ours, and a permanent rival
to us.

Now that we have understood why Islam, the most formidable
of the heresies, achieved its strength and astounding success we
must try to understand why, alone of all the heresies, it has
survived in full strength and even continues (after a fashion) to
expand to this day.

This is a point of decisive importance to the understanding
not only of our subject but of the history of the world in general.
Yet it is one which is, unfortunately, left almost entirely undis-
cussed in the modern world.

Millions of modern people of the white civilization—that is,
the civilization of Europe and America—have forgotten all about
Islam. They have never come in contact with it. They take for
granted that it is decaying, and that, anyway, it is just a foreign
religion which will not concern them. It is, as a fact, the most
formidable and persistent enemy which our civilization has had,
and may at any moment become as large a menace in the future
as it has been in the past.

To that point of its future menace I shall return in the last
of these pages on Mohammedanism.

All the great heresies—save this one of Mohammedanism—
seem to go through the same phases.

First they rise with great violence and become fashionable;
they do so by insisting on some one of the great Catholic doctrines in an exaggerated fashion; and because the great Catholic
doctrines combined form the only full and satisfactory philosophy known to mankind, each doctrine is bound to have its special appeal.

Thus Arianism insisted on the unity of God, combined with
the majesty and creative power of Our Lord. At the same time
it appealed to imperfect minds because it tried to rationalize a
mystery. Calvinism again had a great success because it insisted

on another main doctrine, the Omnipotence and Omniscience of God. It got the rest out of proportion and went violently wrong on Predestination; but it had its moment of triumph when it looked as though it were going to conquer all our civilization—which it would have done if the French had not fought it in their great religious war and conquered its adherents on that soil of Gaul, which has always been the battleground and testing place of European ideas.

After this first phase of the great heresies, when they are in their initial vigor and spread like a flame from man to man, there comes a second phase of decline, lasting, apparently (according to some obscure law), through about five or six generations: say a couple of hundred years or a little more. The adherents of the heresy grow less numerous and less convinced until at last only quite a small number can be called full and faithful followers of the original movement.

Then comes the third phase, when each heresy wholly disappears as a bit of doctrine: no one believes the doctrine any more, or only such a tiny fraction remain believers that they no longer count. But the social and moral factors of the heresy remain and may be of powerful effect for generations more. We see that in the case of Calvinism today. Calvinism produced the Puritan movement and from that there proceeded as a necessary consequence the isolation of the soul, the breakup of corporate social action, unbridled competition and greed, and at last the full establishment of what we call "Industrial Capitalism" today, whereby civilization is now imperilled through the discontent of the vast destitute majority with their few plutocratic masters. There is no one left except perhaps a handful of people in Scotland who really believe the doctrines Calvin taught, but the spirit of Calvinism is still very strong in the countries it originally infected, and its social fruits remain.

Now in the case of Islam none of all this happened except the *first* phase. There was no second phase of gradual decline in the numbers and conviction of its followers. On the contrary, Islam grew from strength to strength acquiring more and more territory, converting more and more followers, until it had established itself as a quite separate civilization and seemed so like a new religion that most people came to forget its origin as a heresy.

Islam increased not only in numbers and in the conviction of its followers, but in territory and in actual political and armed power until close on the eighteenth century. Less than 100 years before the American War of Independence a Mohammedan army was threatening to overrun and destroy Christian civilization, and would have done so if the Catholic King of Poland had not destroyed that army outside Vienna.

Since then the armed power of Mohammedanism has declined; but neither its numbers nor the conviction of its followers have appreciably declined; and as to the territory annexed by it, though it has lost places in which it ruled over subject Christian majorities, it has gained new adherents—to some extent in Asia, and largely in Africa. Indeed in Africa it is still expanding among the negroid populations, and that expansion provides an important future problem for the European Governments who have divided Africa between them.

And there is another point in connection with this power of Islam. Islam is apparently *unconvertible*.

The missionary efforts made by great Catholic orders which have been occupied in trying to turn Mohammedans into Christians for nearly 400 years have everywhere wholly failed. We have in some places driven the Mohammedan master out and freed his Christian subjects from Mohammedan control, but we have had hardly any effect in converting individual Mohammedans save perhaps to some small amount in Southern Spain 500 years ago; and even so, that was rather an example of political than of religious change.

Now what is the explanation of all this? Why should Islam alone of all the great heresies show such continued vitality?

Those who are sympathetic with Mohammedanism and still more those who are actually Mohammedans explain it by proclaiming it the best and most human of religions, the best suited to mankind, and the most attractive.

Strange as it may seem, there are a certain number of highly educated men, European gentlemen, who have actually joined Islam, that is, who are personal converts to Mohammedanism. I myself have known and talked to some half-dozen of them in various parts of the world, and there are a very much larger number of similar men, well-instructed Europeans, who, having lost their faith in Catholicism or in some form of Protestantism in which they were brought up, feel sympathy with the Mohammedan social scheme, although they do not actually join it or profess belief in its religion. We constantly meet men of this kind today among those who have traveled in the East.

These men always give the same answer—Islam is indestructible because it is founded on simplicity and justice. It has kept those Christian doctrines which are evidently true and which appeal to the common sense of millions, while getting rid of priestcraft, mysteries, sacraments, and all the rest of it. It proclaims and practices human equality. It loves justice and forbids usury. It produces a society in which men are happier and feel their own dignity more than in any other. That is its strength and that is why it still converts people and endures and will perhaps return to power in the near future.

Now I do not think that explanation to be the true one. All heresy talks in those terms. Every heresy will tell you that it has purified the corruptions of Christian doctrines and in general done nothing but good to mankind, satisfied the human soul, and so on. Yet every one of them *except* Mohammedanism has faded out. Why?

In order to get the answer to the problem, we must remark in what the fortunes of Islam have differed from those of all the other great heresies, and when we remark that I think we shall have the clue to the truth.

Islam has differed from all the other heresies in two main points which must be carefully noticed:

(1) It did not rise within the Church, that is, within the frontiers of our civilization. Its heresiarch was not a man originally Catholic who led away Catholic followers by his novel doctrine

as did Arius or Calvin. He was an outsider, born a pagan, living among pagans, and never baptized. He adopted Christian doctrines and selected among them in the true heresiarch fashion. He dropped those that did not suit him and insisted on those that did—which is the mark of the heresiarch—but he did not do this as from within; his action was external.

Those first small but fierce armies of nomad Arabs who won their astounding victories in Syria and Egypt against the Catholic world of the early seventh century were made of men who had all been pagans before they became Mohammedan. There was among them no previous Catholicism to which they might return.

(2) This body of Islam attacking Christendom from beyond its frontiers and not breaking it up from within, happened to be continually recruited with fighting material of the strongest kind and drafted in from the pagan outer darkness.

This recruitment went on in waves, incessantly, through the centuries until the end of the Middle Ages. It was mainly Mongol coming from Asia (though some of it was Berber coming from North Africa), and it was this ceaseless, recurrent impact of new adherents, conquerors and fighters as the original Arabs had been, which gave Islam its formidable resistance and continuance of power.

Not long after the first conquest of Syria and Egypt it looked as though the enthusiastic new heresy, in spite of its dazzling sudden triumph, would fail. The continuity in leadership broke down. So did the political unity of the whole scheme. The original capital of the movement was Damascus, and at first Mohammedanism was a Syrian thing (and, by extension, an Egyptian thing); but after quite a short time a breakup was apparent. A new dynasty began ruling from Mesopotamia and no longer from Syria. The Western Districts, that is North Africa and Spain (after the conquest of Spain), formed a separate political government under a separate obedience. *But the caliphs at Baghdad began to support themselves by a bodyguard of hired fighters who were Mongols from the steppes of Asia.*

The characteristic of these nomadic Mongols (who come after the fifth century over and over again in waves to the assault against our civilization), is that they are indomitable fighters and at the same time almost purely destructive. They massacre by the millions; they burn and destroy; they turn fertile districts into deserts. They seem incapable of creative effort.

Twice we in the Christian European West have barely escaped final destruction at their hands; once when we defeated the vast Asiatic army of Attila near Chalons in France, in the middle of the fifth century (not before he had committed horrible out-rage and left ruin behind him everywhere), and again in the thir-teenth century, 800 years later. Then the advancing Asiatic Mongol power was checked, not by our armies but by the death of the man who had united it in his one hand. But it was not checked till it reached north Italy and was approaching Venice.

It was this recruitment of Mongol bodyguards in successive installments which kept Islam going and prevented its suffering the fate that all other heresies had suffered. It kept Islam thun-dering like a battering ram from *outside the frontiers* of Europe, making breaches in our defense and penetrating further and fur-ther into what had been Christian lands.

The Mongol invaders readily accepted Islam; the men who served as mercenary soldiers and formed the real power of the Caliphs were quite ready to conform to the simple requirements of Mohammedanism. They had no regular religion of their own strong enough to counteract the effects of those doctrines of Islam which, mutilated as they were, were in the main Christian doctrines—the unity and majesty of God, the immortality of the soul and all the rest of it. The Mongol mercenaries supporting the political power of the Caliphs were attracted to these main doctrines and easily adopted them. They became good Moslems and as soldiers supporting the Caliphs were thus propagators and maintainers of Islam.

When in the heart of the Middle Ages it looked as though again Islam had failed, a new batch of Mongol soldiers, "Turks" by name, came in and saved the fortunes of Mohammedanism again, although they began by the abominable destruction of such civilization as Mohammedanism had preserved. That is why in the struggles of the Crusades Christians regarded the enemy as "The Turk"; a general name common to many of these nomad tribes. The Christian preachers of the Crusades and captains of the soldiers and the Crusaders in their songs speak of "The Turk" as the enemy, much more than they do in general of Mohammedanism.

In spite of the advantage of being fed by continual recruitment, the pressure of Mohammedanism upon Christendom might have failed after all, had one supreme attempt to relieve that pressure upon the Christian West succeeded. That supreme attempt was made in the middle of the whole business (A.D. 1095-1200) and is called in history "The Crusades." Catholic Christendom succeeded in recapturing Spain; it nearly succeeded in pushing back Mohammedanism from Syria, in saving the Christian civilization of Asia, and in cutting off the Asiatic Mohammedan from the African. Had it done so, perhaps Mohammedanism would have died.

But the Crusades failed. Their failure is the major tragedy in the history of our struggle against Islam, that is, against Asia—against the East.

What the Crusades were, and why and how they failed I shall now describe.

The success of Mohammedanism had not been due to its offering something more satisfactory in the way of philosophy and morals, but, as I have said, to the opportunity it afforded of freedom to the slave and debtor, and an extreme simplicity which pleased the unintelligent masses who were perplexed by the mysteries inseparable from the profound intellectual life of Catholicism, and from its radical doctrine of the Incarnation. But it was spreading, and it looked as though it were bound to win universally, as do all great heresies in their beginnings, because it was the fashionable thing of the time—the conquering thing.

Now against the great heresies, when they acquire the driving power of being the new and fashionable thing, there arises a reaction within the Christian and Catholic mind, which reaction gradually turns the current backward, gets rid of the poison and re-establishes Christian civilization. Such reactions, begin, I repeat, obscurely. It is the plain man who gets uncomfortable and says to himself, "This may be the fashion of the moment, but I don't like it." It is the mass of Christian men who feel in their bones that there is something wrong, though they have difficulty in explaining it. The reaction is usually slow and muddled and for a long time not successful. But in the long run with internal heresy it has always succeeded; just as the native health of the human body succeeds in getting rid of some internal infection.

A heresy, when it is full of its original power, affects even Catholic thought—thus Arianism produced a mass of semi-Arianism running throughout Christendom. The Manichean dread of the body and the false doctrine that matter is evil affected even the greatest Catholics of the time. There is a touch of it in the letters of the great St. Gregory. In the same way Mohammedanism had its effect on the Christian Emperors of Byzantium and on Charlemagne, the Emperor of the West; for instance, there was a powerful movement started against the use of images, which are so essential to Catholic worship. Even in the West, where Mohammedanism had never reached, the attempt to get rid of images in the churches nearly succeeded.

But while Mohammedanism was spreading, absorbing greater and greater numbers into its own body out of the subject Christian populations of East and North Africa, occupying more and more territory, a defensive reaction against it had begun. Islam gradually absorbed North Africa and crossed over into Spain; less than a century after those first victories in Syria it even pushed across the Pyrenees, right into France. Luckily it was defeated in battle halfway between Tours and Poitiers in the north center of the country. Some think that if the Christian leaders had not won that battle, the whole of Christendom would have been swamped by Mohammedanism. At any rate, from that moment in the West it never advanced further. It was pushed back to the Pyrenees, and very slowly indeed over a period of 300 years it was thrust further and further south towards the center of Spain, the north of which was cleared again of Mohammedan influence. In the East, however, as we shall see, it continued to be an overwhelming threat.

Now the success of Christian men in pushing back the Mohammedan from France and halfway down Spain began a sort of re-awakening in Europe. It was high time. We of the West had been besieged in three ways; pagan Asiatics had come upon us in the very heart of the Germanies; pagan pirates of the most cruel and disgusting sort had swarmed over the Northern Seas and nearly wiped out Christian civilization in England and hurt it also in Northern France; and with all that there had been this pressure of Mohammedanism coming from the South and Southeast—a much more civilized pressure than that of the Asiatics or Scandinavian pirates but still a menace, under which our Christian civilization came near to disappearing.

It is most interesting to take a map of Europe and mark off the extreme limits reached by the enemies of Christendom during the worst of this struggle for existence. The outriders of the worst Asiatic raid got as far as Tournus on the Saône, which is in the very middle of what is France today; the Mohammedan got, as we have seen, to the very middle of France also, somewhere between Tournus and Poitiers. The horrible Scandinavian pagan pirates raided Ireland, all England, and came up all the rivers of Northern France and Northern Germany. They got as far as Cologne, they besieged Paris, they nearly took Hamburg. People today forget how very doubtful a thing it was in the height of the Dark Ages, between the middle of the eighth and the end of the ninth century, whether Catholic civilization would survive at all. Half the Mediterranean Islands had fallen to the Mohammedan, all the Near East; he was fighting to get hold of Asia Minor; and the north and center of Europe were perpetually raided by the Asiatics and the Northern pagans.

Then came the great reaction and the awakening of Europe. The chivalry which poured out of Gaul into Spain and the native Spanish knights forcing back the Mohammedans began the affair. The Scandinavian pirates and the raiders from Asia had been defeated two generations before. Pilgrimages to Jerusalem, distant, expensive and perilous, but continuous throughout the Dark Ages, were now especially imperilled through a new Mongol wave of Mohammedan soldiers establishing themselves over the East and especially in Palestine; and the cry arose that the Holy Places, the True Cross (which was preserved in Jerusalem) and the remaining Christian communities of Syria and Palestine, and above all the Holy Sepulchre—the site of the Resurrection, the main object of every pilgrimage—ought to be saved from the usurping hands of Islam. Enthusiastic men preached the duty of marching eastward and rescuing the Holy Land; the reigning Pope, Urban, put himself at the head of the movement in a famous sermon delivered in France to vast crowds, who cried out: "God wills it." Irregular bodies began to pour out eastward for the thrusting back of Islam from the Holy Land, and in due time the regular levies of great Christian Princes prepared for an organized effort on a vast scale. Those who vowed themselves to pursue the effort took the badge of the Cross on their clothing, and from this the struggle became to be known as the Crusades.

The First Crusade was launched in three great bodies of more or less organized Christian soldiery, who set out to march from Western Europe to the Holy Land. I say "more or less organized" because the feudal army was never highly organized; it was divided into units of very different sizes each following a feudal lord—but of course it had sufficient organization to carry a military enterprise through, because a mere herd of men can never do that. In order not to exhaust the provisions of the countries through which they had to march, the Christian leaders went in three bodies, one from Northern France, going down the valley of the Danube; another from Southern France, going across Italy; and a third of Frenchmen who had recently acquired dominion in Southern Italy and who crossed the Adriatic directly, making for Constantinople through the Balkans. They all joined at Constantinople, and by the time they got there,

there were still in spite of losses on the way something which may have been a quarter of a million men—perhaps more. The numbers were never accurately known or computed.

The Emperor at Constantinople was still free, at the head of his great Christian capital, but he was dangerously menaced by the fighting Mohammedan Turks who were only just over the water in Asia Minor, and whose object it was to get hold of Constantinople and so press on to the ruin of Christendom. This pressure on Constantinople the great mass of the Crusaders immediately relieved; they won a battle against the Turks at Dorylaeum and pressed on with great difficulty and further large losses of men till they reached the corner where Syria joins on to Asia Minor at the Gulf of Alexandretta. There, one of the Crusading leaders carved out a kingdom for himself, making his capital at the Christian town of Edessa, to serve as a bulwark against further Mohammedan pressure from the East. The last of the now dwindling Christian forces besieged and with great difficulty took Antioch, which the Mohammedans had got hold of a few years before. Here another Crusading leader made himself feudal lord, and there was a long delay and a bad quarrel between the Crusaders and the Emperor of Constantinople, who naturally wanted them to return to him what had been portions of his realm before Mohammedanism had grown up—while the Crusaders wanted to keep what they had conquered so that the revenues might become an income for each of them.

At last they got away from Antioch at the beginning of the open season of the third year after they had started—the last year of the eleventh century, 1099; they took all the towns along the coast as they marched; when they got on a level with Jerusalem they struck inland and stormed the city on the 15th of July of that year, killing all the Mohammedan garrison and establishing themselves firmly within the walls of the Holy City. They then organized their capture into a feudal kingdom, making one of their number titular King of the new realm of Jerusalem. They chose for that office a great noble of the country where the Teutonic and Gallic races meet in the northeast of France—Godfrey of Bouillon, a powerful Lord of the Marches. He had under him as nominal inferiors the great feudal lords who had carved out districts for themselves from Edessa southwards, and those who had built and established themselves in the great stone castles which still remain, among the finest ruins in the world.

By the time the Crusaders had accomplished their object and seized the Holy Places, they had dwindled to a very small number of men. It is probable that the actual fighting men, as distinguished from servants, camp followers and the rest, present at the siege of Jerusalem, did not count much more than 15,000. And upon that force everything turned. Syria had not been thoroughly recovered, nor the Mohammedans finally thrust back; the seacoast was held with the support of a population still largely Christian, but the plain and the seacoast and Palestine up to the Jordan make only a narrow strip behind which and parallel to which comes a range of hills which in the middle of the country are great mountains—the Lebanon and the Anti-Lebanon. Behind that again the country turns into desert, and on the edge of the desert there is a string of towns which are, as it were, the ports of the desert—that is, the points where the caravans arrive.

These "ports of the desert" have always been rendered very important by commerce, and their names go back well beyond the beginning of recorded history. A string of towns thus stretched along the edge of the desert begins from Aleppo in the north down as far as Petra, south of the Dead Sea. They were united by the great caravan route which reaches to North Arabia, and they were all predominantly Mohammedan by the time of the Crusading effort. The central one of these towns and the richest, the great market of Syria, is Damascus. If the first Crusaders had had enough men to take Damascus, their effort would have been permanently successful. But their forces were insufficient for that, they could only barely hold the seacoast of Palestine up to the Jordan—and even so, they held it only by the aid of immense fortified works.

There was a good deal of commerce with Europe, but not

sufficient recruitment of forces, and the consequence was that the vast sea of Mohammedanism all around began to seep in and undermine the Christian position. The first sign of what was coming was the fall of Edessa (the capital of the northeastern state of the Crusading federation, the state most exposed to attack), less than half a century after the first capture of Jerusalem.

It was the first serious setback, and roused great excitement in the Christian West. The Kings of France and England set out with great armies to re-establish the Crusading position, and this time they went for the strategic key of the whole country—Damascus. But they failed to take it: and when they and their men sailed back again, the position of the Crusaders in Syria was as perilous as it had been before. They were guaranteed another lease of precarious security as long as the Mohammedan world was divided into rival bodies, but it was certain that if ever a leader should arise who could unify the Mohammedan power in his hands the little Christian garrisons were doomed.

And this is exactly what happened. Salah-ed-Din—whom we call Saladin—a soldier of genius, the son of a former Governor of Damascus, gradually acquired all power over the Mohammedan world of the Near East. He became master of all Egypt, master of the towns on the fringe of the desert, and when he marched to the attack with his united forces the remaining Christian body of Syria had no chance of victory. They made a fine rally, withdrawing every available man from their castle garrisons and forming a mobile force which attempted to relieve the siege of the castle of Tiberias on the Sea of Galilee. The Christian Army was approaching Tiberias and had got as far as the sloping mountainside of Hattin, about a day's march away, when it was attacked by Saladin and destroyed.

That disaster, which took place in the summer of 1187, was followed by the collapse of nearly the whole Christian military colony in Syria and the Holy Land. Saladin took town after town, save one or two points on the seacoast which were to remain in Christian hands more than another lifetime. But the kingdom of Jerusalem, the feudal Christian realm which had recovered and held the Holy Places, was gone. Jerusalem itself fell of course, and its fall produced an enormous effect in Europe. All the great leaders, the King of England, Richard Plantagenet, the King of France and the Emperor, commanding jointly a large and first-rate army mainly German in recruitment, all set out to recover what had been lost. But they failed. They managed to get hold of one or two more points on the coast, but they never retook Jerusalem and never re-established the old Christian kingdom.

Thus ended a series of three mighty duels between Christendom and Islam. Islam had won.

Had the Crusaders' remaining force at the end of the first Crusading march been a little more numerous, had they taken Damascus and the string of towns on the fringe of the desert, the whole history of the world would have been changed. The world of Islam would have been cut in two, with the East unable to approach the West; probably we Europeans would have recovered North Africa and Egypt—we should certainly have saved Constantinople—and Mohammedanism would only have survived as an Oriental religion thrust beyond the ancient boundaries of the Roman Empire. As it was, Mohammedanism not only survived but grew stronger. It was indeed slowly thrust out of Spain and the eastern islands of the Mediterranean, but it maintained its hold on the whole of North Africa, Syria, Palestine, Asia Minor, and thence it went forward and conquered the Balkans and Greece, overran Hungary and twice threatened to overrun Germany and reach France again from the East, putting an end to our civilization. One of the reasons that the breakdown of Christendom at the Reformation took place was the fact that Mohammedan pressure against the German Emperor gave the German Princes and towns the opportunity to rebel and start Protestant Churches in their dominions.

Many expeditions followed against the Turk in one form or another; they were called Crusades, and the idea continued until the very end of the Middle Ages. But there was no recovery of Syria and no thrusting back of the Moslem.

Meanwhile the first Crusading march had brought so many new experiences to Western Europe that culture had developed very rapidly and produced the magnificent architecture and the high philosophy and social structure of the Middle Ages. That was the real fruit of the Crusades. They failed in their own field, but they made modern Europe. Yet they made it at the expense of the old idea of Christian unity; with increasing material civilization, modern nations began to form, Christendom still held together, but it held together loosely. At last came the storm of the Reformation; Christendom broke up, the various nations and Princes claimed to be independent of any common control such as the moral position of the Papacy had insured, and we slid down that slope which was to end at last in the wholesale massacre of modern war—which may prove the destruction of our civilization. Napoleon Bonaparte very well said: *Every war in Europe is really a civil war.* It is profoundly true. Christian Europe is and should be by nature one; but it has forgotten its nature in forgetting its religion.

The last subject but one in our appreciation of the great Mohammedan attack upon the Catholic Church and the civilization she had produced, is the sudden last effort and subsequent rapid decline of Mohammedan political power just after it had reached its summit. The last subject of all in this connection, the one which I will treat next, is the very important and almost neglected question of whether Mohammedan power may not rearise in the modern world.

If we recapitulate the fortunes of Islam after its triumph in beating back the Crusaders and restoring its dominion over the East and confirming its increasing grasp over half of what had once been a united Graeco-Roman Christendom, Islam proceeded to develop two completely different and even contradictory fortunes: it was gradually losing its hold on Western Europe while it was increasing its hold over Southeastern Europe.

In Spain it had already been beaten back halfway from the Pyrenees to the Straits of Gibraltar before the Crusades were launched and it was destined in the next four to five centuries to lose every inch of ground which it had governed in the Iberian Peninsula: today called "Spain and Portugal." Continental Western Europe (and even the islands attached to it) was cleared of Mohammedan influence during the last centuries of the Middle Ages, the twelfth to fifteenth centuries.

This was because the Mohammedans of the West, that is, what was then called "Barbary," what is now French and Italian North Africa, were politically separated from the vast majority of the Mohammedan world which lay to the East.

Between the Barbary states (which we call today Tunis, Algiers and Morocco) and Egypt, the desert made a barrier difficult to cross. The West was less barren in former times than it is today, and the Italians are reviving its prosperity. But the vast stretches of sand and gravel, with very little water, always made this barrier between Egypt and the West a deterrent and an obstacle. Yet, more important than this barrier was the gradual disassociation between the Western Mohammedans of North Africa and the mass of Mohammedans to the East thereof. The religion indeed remained the same, and the social habits and all the rest. Mohammedanism in North Africa remained one world with Mohammedanism in Syria, Asia and Egypt, just as the Christian civilization in the West of Europe remained for long one world with the Christian civilization of Central Europe and even of Eastern Europe. But distance and the fact that the Eastern Mohammedans never sufficiently came to their help made the Western Mohammedans of North Africa and of Spain feel themselves something separate politically from their Eastern brethren.

To this we must add the factor of *distance* and its effect on sea power in those days and in those waters. The Mediterranean is much more than two thousand miles long; the only period of the year in which any effective fighting could be done on its waters under medieval conditions was the late spring, summer and early autumn, and it is precisely in those five months of the year, when alone men could use the Mediterranean for great expeditions, that offensive military operations were handicapped by long calms. It is true these were met by the use of many-oared galleys so as to make fleets as little dependent on wind as possible, but still, distances of that kind did make unity of action difficult.

Therefore, the Mohammedans of North Africa not being supported at sea by the wealth and numbers of their brethren from the ports of Asia Minor and of Syria and the mouths of the Nile, gradually lost control of maritime communications. They lost, therefore, the Western islands, Sicily and Corsica and Sardinia, the Balearics and even Malta at the very moment when they were triumphantly capturing the Eastern islands in the Aegean Sea. The only form of sea power remaining to the Mohammedan in the West was the active piracy of the Algerian sailors operating from the lagoon of Tunis and half-sheltered bay of Algiers. (The word "Algiers" comes from the Arabic word for "islands." There was no proper harbor before the French conquest of a hundred years ago, but there was a roadstead partially sheltered by a string of rocks and islets.) These pirates remained a peril right on until the seventeenth century. It is interesting to notice, for instance, that the Mohammedan call to prayer was heard on the coasts of Southern Ireland within the lifetime of Oliver Cromwell, for the Algerian pirates departed from everywhere, not only in the Western Mediterranean but along the coasts of the Atlantic, from the Straits of Gibraltar to the English Channel. They were no longer capable of conquest, but they could loot and take prisoners whom they held to ransom.

While this beating back of the Mohammedan into Africa was going on to the western side of Europe, exactly the opposite was happening on the *eastern* side. After the Crusades had failed Mohammedans made themselves secure in Asia Minor and began that long hammering at Constantinople which finally succeeded.

Constantinople was by far the richest and greatest capital of the Ancient World; it was the old center of Greek and Roman civilization, and even when it had lost all direct political power over Italy—and still more over France—it continued to be revered as the mighty monument of the Roman past. The Emperor of Constantinople was the direct heir of the Caesars. On the military side this very strong city, supported by great masses of tribute and by a closely knit, well disciplined army, was the bulwark of Christendom. So long as Constantinople stood as a Christian city and Mass was still said in St. Sophia, the doors of Europe were locked against Islam. It fell in the same generation that saw the expulsion of the last Mohammedan government from southern Spain. Men who in their maturity marched into Granada with the victorious armies of Isabella the Catholic could remember how, in early childhood, they had heard the awful news that Constantinople itself had fallen to the enemies of the Church.

The fall of Constantinople at the end of the Middle Ages (1453) was only the beginning of further Mohammedan advances. Islam swept all over the Balkans; it took all the eastern Mediterranean islands, Crete and Rhodes and the rest; it completely occupied Greece; it began pushing up the Danube valley and northwards into the great plains; it destroyed the ancient kingdom of Hungary in the fatal battle of Mohacs and at last, in the first third of the sixteenth century, just at the moment when the storm of the Reformation had broken out, Islam threatened Europe close at hand, bringing pressure upon the heart of the Empire, at Vienna.

It is not generally appreciated how the success of Luther's religious revolution against Catholicism in Germany was due to the way in which Mohammedan pressure from the East was paralyzing the central authority of the German Emperors. They had to compromise with the leaders of the religious revolution and try to patch up a sort of awkward peace between the irreconcilable claims of Catholic authority and Protestant religious theory in order to meet the enemy at their gates; the enemy which had already overthrown Hungary and might well overthrow all Southern Germany and perhaps reach the Rhine. If Islam had succeeded in doing this during the chaos of violent civil dissension among the Germans, due to the launching of the Reformation, our civilization would have been as effectively destroyed as it would have been if the first rush of the Mohammedans through Spain had not been checked and beaten back eight centuries earlier in the middle of France.

This violent Mohammedan pressure on Christendom from the East made a bid for success by sea as well as by land. The last great wave of Mongol soldiery, the last great Turkish organization working now from the conquered capital of Constantinople, proposed to cross the Adriatic, to attack Italy by sea and ultimately to recover all that had been lost in the Western Mediterranean.

There was one critical moment when it looked as though the scheme would succeed. A huge Mohammedan armada fought at the mouth of the Gulf of Corinth against the Christian fleet at Lepanto. The Christians won that naval action, and the Western Mediterranean was saved. But it was a very close thing, and the name of Lepanto should remain in the minds of all men with a sense of history as one of the half dozen great names in the history of the Christian world. It has been a worthy theme for the finest battle poem of our time, "The Ballad of Lepanto," by the late Mr. Gilbert Chesterton.

Today we are accustomed to think of the Mohammedan world as something backward and stagnant, in all material affairs at least. We cannot imagine a great Mohammedan fleet made up of modern ironclads and submarines, or a great modern Mohammedan army fully equipped with modern artillery, flying power and the rest. But not so very long ago, *less than a hundred years before the Declaration of Independence,* the Mohammedan Government centered at Constantinople had better artillery and better army equipment of every kind than had we Christians in the West. The last effort they made to destroy Christendom was contemporary with the end of the reign of Charles II in England and of his brother James and of the usurper William III. It failed during the last years of the seventeeth century, only just over two hundred years ago. Vienna, as we saw, was almost taken and only saved by the Christian army under the command of the King of Poland on a date that ought to be among the most famous in history—September 11, 1683. But the peril remained, Islam was still immensely powerful within a few marches of Austria and it was not until the great victory of Prince Eugene at Zenta in 1697 and the capture of Belgrade that the tide really turned—and by that time we were at the end of the seventeenth century.

It should be fully grasped that the generation of Dean Swift, the men who saw the court of Louis XIV in old age, the men who saw the Hanoverians brought in as puppet Kings for England by the dominating English wealthy class, the men who saw the apparent extinction of Irish freedom after the failure of James II's campaign at the Boyne and the later surrender of Limerick, all that lifetime which overlapped between the end of the seventeenth and the beginning of the eighteenth century, was dominated by a vivid memory of a Mohammedan threat which had very nearly made good and which apparently might in the near future be repeated. The Europeans of that time thought of Mohammedanism as we think of Bolshevism or as white men in Asia think of Japanese power today.

What happened was something quite unexpected; the Mohammedan power began to break down on the material side. The Mohammedans lost the power of competing successfully with the Christians in the making of those instruments whereby dominion is assured; armament, methods of communication and all the rest of it. Not only did they not advance, they went back. Their artillery became much worse than ours. While our use of the sea vastly increased, theirs sank away till they had no first-class ships with which to fight naval battles.

The eighteenth century is a story of their gradual losing of the race against the European in material things.

When that vast revolution in human affairs introduced by the invention of modern machinery began in England and spread slowly throughout Europe, the Mohammedan world proved itself quite incapable of taking advantage thereof. During the Napoleonic wars, although supported by England, Islam failed entirely to meet the French armies of Egypt; its last effort resulted in complete defeat (the land battle of the Nile).

All during the nineteenth century the process continued. As a result, Mohammedan North Africa was gradually subjected to European control, the last independent piece to go being Morocco. Egypt fell under the control of England. Long before that Greece had been liberated, and the Balkan states. Half a lifetime ago it was taken for granted everywhere that the last remnants of Mohammedan power in Europe would disappear. England bolstered it up and did save Constantinople from being taken by the Russians in 1877-78, but it seemed only a question of a few years before the Turks would be wiped out for good. Everyone was waiting for the end of Islam, on this side of the Bosphorus at least; while in Syria, Asia Minor and Mesopotamia it was losing all political and military vigor. After the Great War, what was left of Mohammedan power, even in hither Asia, let alone in Constantinople, was only saved by the violent quarrels between the Allies.

Even Syria and Palestine were divided between France and England. Mesopotamia fell under the control of England and no menace of Islamic power remained, though it was still entrenched in Asia Minor and kept a sort of precarious hold on the thoroughly decayed city of Constantinople alone. The Mediterranean was gone; every inch of European territory was gone; and the great duel between Islam and Christendom seemed at last to have been decided in our own day.

To what was due this collapse? I have never seen an answer to that question. There was no moral disintegration from within, there was no intellectual breakdown; you will find the Egyptian or Syrian student today, if you talk to him on any philosophical or scientific subject which he has studied, to be the equal of any European. If Islam has no physical science now applied to any of its problems, in arms and communications, it has apparently ceased to be part of our world and fallen definitely below it. Of every dozen Mohammedans in the world today, eleven are actually or virtually subjects of an Occidental power. It would seem, I repeat, as though the great duel was now decided.

But can we be certain it is so decided? I doubt it very much. It has always seemed to me possible, and even probable, that there would be a resurrection of Islam and that our sons or our grandsons would see the renewal of that tremendous struggle between the Christian culture and what has been for more than a thousand years its greatest opponent.

Why this conviction should have arisen in the minds of certain observers and travellers, such as myself, I will now consider. It is indeed a vital question, "May not Islam rise again?"

In a sense the question is already answered because Islam has never departed. It still commands the fixed loyalty and unquestioning adhesion of all the millions between the Atlantic and the Indus and further afield throughout scattered communities of further Asia. But I ask the question in the sense, "Will not perhaps the temporal power of Islam return and with it the menace of an armed Mohammedan world which will shake off the domination of Europeans—still nominally Christian—and reappear again as the prime enemy of our civilization?" The future always comes as a surprise, but political wisdom consists in attempting at least some partial judgment of what that surprise may be. And for my part I cannot but believe that a main unexpected thing of the future is the return of Islam. Since religion is at the root of all political movements and changes and since we have here a very great religion physically paralyzed but morally intensely alive, we are in the presence of an unstable equilibrium which cannot remain permanently unstable. Let us then examine the position.

I have said throughout these pages that the particular quality of Mohammedanism, regarded as a heresy, was its vitality. Alone of all the great heresies Mohammedanism struck permanent roots, developing a life of its own, and became at last something like a new religion. So true is this that today very few men, even among those who are highly instructed in history, recall the truth that Mohammedanism was essentially in its origins *not* a new religion, but a *heresy*.

Like all heresies, Mohammedanism lived by the Catholic truths which it had retained. Its insistence on personal immortality, on the Unity and Infinite Majesty of God, on His Justice and Mercy, its insistence on the equality of human souls in the sight of their Creator—these are its strength.

But it has survived for other reasons than these; all the other great heresies had their truths as well as their falsehoods and vagaries, yet they have died one after the other. The Catholic Church has seen them pass, and though their evil consequences are still with us the heresies themselves are dead.

The strength of Calvinism was the truth on which it insisted, the Omnipotence of God, the dependence and insufficiency of man; but its error, which was the negation of free-will, also killed it. For men could not permanently accept so monstrous a denial of common sense and common experience. Arianism lived by the truth that was in it, to wit, the fact that the reason could not directly reconcile the opposite aspects of a great mystery—that of the Incarnation. But Arianism died because it added to this truth a falsehood, to wit, that the apparent contradiction could be solved by denying the full Divinity of Our Lord.

And so on with the other heresies. But Mohammedanism, though it also contained errors side by side with those great truths, flourished continually, *and as a body of doctrine is flourishing still,* though thirteen hundred years have passed since its first great victories in Syria. The causes of this vitality are very difficult to explore, and perhaps cannot be reached. For myself I should ascribe it in some part to the fact that Mohammedanism being a thing from outside, a heresy that did not arise with the body of the Christian community but beyond its frontiers, has always possessed a reservoir of men, newcomers pouring in to revivify its energies. But that cannot be a full explanation; perhaps Mohammedanism would have died but for the successive waves of recruitment from the desert and from Asia; perhaps it would have died if the Caliphate at Baghdad had been left entirely to itself, and if the Moors in the West had not been able to draw upon continual recruitment from the South.

Whatever the cause be, Mohammedanism has survived, and vigorously survived. Missionary effort has had no appreciable effect upon it. It still converts pagan savages wholesale. It even attracts from time to time some European eccentric, who joins its body. *But the Mohammedan never becomes a Catholic.* No fragment of Islam ever abandons its sacred book, its code of morals, its organized system of prayer, its simple doctrine.

In view of this, anyone with a knowledge of history is bound to ask himself whether we shall not see in the future a revival of Mohammedan political power, and the renewal of the old pressure of Islam upon Christendom.

We have seen how the material political power of Islam declined very rapidly during the eighteenth and nineteenth centuries. We have just followed the story of that decline. When Suleiman the Magnificent was besieging Vienna he had better artillery, better energies and better everything than his opponents; Islam was still in the field the material superior of Christendom—at least it was the superior in fighting power and fighting instruments. That was within a very few years of the opening of the eighteenth century. Then came the inexplicable decline. The religion did not decay, but its political power and with that its material power declined astonishingly, and in the particular business of arms it declined most of all. When Dr. Johnson's father, the bookseller, was setting up in business at Lichfield, the Grand Turk was still dreaded as a potential conqueror of Europe; before Dr. Johnson was dead, no Turkish fleet or army could trouble the West. Not a lifetime later, the Mohammedan in North Africa had fallen subject to the French; and those who were then young men lived to see nearly all Mohammedan territory, except for a decaying fragment ruled from Constantinople, firmly subdued by the French and British Governments.

These things being so, the recrudescence of Islam, the possibility of that terror under which we lived for centuries reappearing, and of our civilization again fighting for its life against what was its chief enemy for a thousand years, seems fantastic. Who in the Mohammedan world today can manufacture and maintain the complicated instruments of modern war? Where is the political machinery whereby the religion of Islam can play an equal part in the modern world?

I say the suggestion that Islam may re-arise sounds fantastic—but this is only because men are always powerfully affected by the immediate past:—one might say that they are blinded by it.

Cultures spring from religions; ultimately the vital force which maintains any culture is its philosophy, its attitude towards the universe; the decay of a religion involves the decay of the culture corresponding to it—we see that most clearly in the breakdown of Christendom today. The bad work begun at the Reformation is bearing its final fruit in the dissolution of our ancestral doctrines—the very structure of our society is dissolving.

In place of the old Christian enthusiasms of Europe there came, for a time, the enthusiasm for nationality, the religion of patriotism. But self-worship is not enough, and the forces which are making for the destruction of our culture, notably the Jewish Communist propaganda from Moscow, have a likelier future before them than our old-fashioned patriotisms.

In Islam there has been no such dissolution of ancestral doctrine—or, at any rate, nothing corresponding to the universal break-up of religion in Europe. The whole spiritual strength of Islam is still present in the masses of Syria and Anatolia, of the East Asian mountains, of Arabia, Egypt and North Africa.

The final fruit of this tenacity, the second period of Islamic power, may be delayed:—but I doubt whether it can be permanently postponed.

There is nothing in the Mohammedan civilization itself which is hostile to the development of scientific knowledge or of mechanical aptitude. I have seen some good artillery work in the hands of Mohammedan students of that arm; I have seen some of the best driving and maintenance of mechanical road transport conducted by Mohammedans. There is nothing inherent to Mohammedanism to make it incapable of modern science and modern war. Indeed, the matter is not worth discussing. It should be self-evident to anyone who has seen the Mohammedan culture at work. That culture happens to have fallen back in material applications; there is no reason whatever why it should not learn its new lesson and become our equal in all those temporal things which now *alone* give us our superiority over it—whereas in *Faith* we have fallen inferior to it.

People who question this may be misled by a number of false suggestions dating from the immediate past. For instance, it was a common saying during the nineteenth century that Mohammedanism had lost its political power through its doctrine of fatalism. But that doctrine was in full vigor when the Mohammedan power was at its height. For that matter, Mohammedanism is no more fatalist than Calvinism; the two heresies resemble each other exactly in their exaggerated insistence upon the immutability of divine decrees.

There was another more intelligent suggestion made in the nineteenth century, which was this: that the decline of Islam had proceeded from its fatal habit of perpetual civil division: the splitting up and changeability of political authority among the Mohammedans. But that weakness of theirs was present from the beginning; it is inherent in the very nature of the Arabian temperament from which they started. Over and over again this individualism of theirs, this "fissiparous" tendency of theirs, has gravely weakened them; yet over and over again they have suddenly united under a leader and accomplished the greatest things.

Now it is probable enough that on these lines—unity under a leader—the return of Islam may arrive. There is no leader as yet, but enthusiasm might bring one and there are signs enough in the political heavens today of what we may have to expect from the revolt of Islam at some future date—perhaps not far distant.

After the Great War, the Turkish power was suddenly restored by one such man. Another such man in Arabia, with equal suddenness, affirmed himself and destroyed all the plans laid for the incorporation of that part of the Mohammedan world into the English sphere. Syria, which is the connecting link, the hinge and the pivot of the whole Mohammedan world, is, upon the map, and superficially, divided between an English and a French mandate; but the two Powers intrigue one against the other and are equally detested by their Mohammedan subjects, who are only kept down precariously by force. There has been bloodshed under the French mandate more than once and it will be renewed,[5] while under the English mandate the forcing of an alien Jewish colony upon Palestine has raised the animosity of the native Arab population to white heat. Meanwhile an ubiquitous underground Bolshevist propaganda is working throughout Syria and North Africa continually, against the domination of Europeans over the original Mohammedan population.

Lastly, there is this further point to which attention should be paid: the attachment (such as it is) of the Mohammedan world in India to English rule is founded mainly upon the gulf between the Mohammedan and the Hindu religions. Every step towards a larger political independence for either party strengthens the Mohammedan desire for renewed power. The Indian Mohammedan will more and more tend to say: "If I am to look after myself and not to be favored as I have been in the past by the alien European master in India—which I once ruled—I will rely upon the revival of Islam." For all these reasons (and many more might be added) men of foresight might justly apprehend, or at any rate expect, the return of Islam.

It would seem as though the Great Heresies were granted an effect proportionate to the lateness of their appearance in the story of Christendom.

The earlier heresies on the Incarnation, when they died out, left no enduring relic of their presence. Arianism was revived for a moment in the general chaos of the Reformation. Sundry scholars, including Milton in England and presumably Bruno in Italy and a whole group of Frenchmen put forward doctrines

---

5. Written in March, 1936.

in the sixteenth and seventeenth centuries which attempted to reconcile a modified materialism and a denial of the Trinity with some part of Christian religion. Milton's effort was particularly noticeable. English official history has, of course, suppressed it as much as possible, by the usual method of scamping all emphasis upon it. The English historians do not deny Milton's materialism; quite recently several English writers on Milton have discoursed at length on his refusal of full divinity to Our Lord. But this effort at suppression will break down, for one cannot forever hide a thing so important as Milton's attack, not only on the Incarnation, but on the Creation, and on the omnipotence of Almighty God.

But of that I will speak later when we come to the Protestant movement. It remains generally true that the earliest heresies not only died out, but left no enduring memorial of their action on European society.

But Mohammedanism coming as much later than Arianism as Arianism was later than the Apostles has left a profound effect on the political structure of Europe and upon language: even to some extent on science.

Politically, it destroyed the independence of the Eastern Empire and though various fragments have, some of them, revived in maimed fashion, the glory and unity of Byzantine rule disappeared forever under the attacks of Islam. The Russian Tsardom, oddly enough, took over a maimed inheritance from Byzantium, but it was a very poor reflection of the old Greek splendor. The truth is that Islam permanently wounded the east of our civilization in such fashion that barbarism partly returned. On North Africa its affect was almost absolute and remains so to this day. Europe has been quite unable to reassert herself there. The great Greek tradition has utterly vanished from the Valley of the Nile and from the Delta, unless one calls Alexandria some sort of relic thereof, with its mainly European civilization, French and Italian, but beyond that right up to the Atlantic the old order failed, apparently forever. The French in taking over the administration of Barbary and planting therein a considerable body of their own colonists, of Spaniards, and of

Italians, have left the main structure of North African society wholly Mohammedan; and there is no sign of its becoming anything else.

In what measure Islam affected our science and our philosophy is open to debate. Its effect has been, of course, heavily exaggerated, because to exaggerate it was a form of attack upon Catholicism. The main part of what writers on mathematics, physical science and geography, from the Islamic side, writers who wrote in Arabic, who professed either the full doctrine of Islam or some heretical form of it (sometimes almost atheist) was drawn from the Greek and Roman civilization which Islam had overwhelmed. It remains true that Islam handed on through such writers a great part of the advances in those departments of knowledge which the Graeco-Roman civilization had made.

During the Dark Ages and even during the early Middle Ages, or at any rate the very early Middle Ages, the Mohammedan world detained the better part of academic teaching and we had to turn to it for our own instruction.

The effect of Mohammedanism on Christian language, though of course a superficial matter, is remarkable. We find it in a host of words, including such very familiar ones as "algebra," "alcohol," "admiral," etc. We find it in the terms of heraldry, and we find it abundantly in place names. Indeed, it is remarkable to see how place names of Roman and Greek origin have been replaced by totally different Semitic terms. Half the rivers of Spain, especially in the southern part of the country, include the term "wadi," and it is curious to note how far in the Western Hemisphere "Guadeloupe" preserves an Arabic form drawn from Estremadura.

The towns in North Africa and the villages for that matter as a rule were rebaptized; the names of the most famous—for instance, Carthage and Caesarea, disappeared. Others arose spontaneously, such as "Algiers," a name derived from the Arabic phrase for "the islands"—the old roadstead of Algiers owing its partial security to a line of rocky islets parallel with the coast.

The whole story of this replacing of the original names of towns and rivers by Semitic forms is one of the most valuable examples we have of the *dis*connection between language and race. The race in North Africa from Libya westward is much what it has been from the beginning of recorded time. It is Berber. Yet the Berber language survives only in a few hill districts and in desert tribes. The Punic, the Greek, the Latin, the common speech of Tripoli (a surviving Greek name, by the way), Tunis, and all Barbary, have quite gone. Such an example should have given pause to the academic theorists who talked of the English as "Anglo-Saxon," and argued from their place names that the English had come over from North Germany and Denmark in little boats, exterminated everybody east of Cornwall and replanted it with their own communities. Yet of such fantasies a good deal survives, most strongly, of course, at Oxford and Cambridge.

5

THE ALBIGENSIAN ATTACK

In the heart of the Middle Ages, just when they were working up to their most splendid phase, the great thirteenth century, there arose—and was for the moment completely defeated—a singular and powerful attack upon the Catholic Church and all the culture for which it stood.

This was an attack, not only on the religion that made our civilization, but on that civilization itself; and its general name in history is "The Albigensian Heresy."

In the case of this great struggle we must proceed as in the case of all our other examples, by first examining the nature of the doctrine which was set up against the body of truth taught by the Catholic Church.

The false doctrine of which the Albigensians were a main example has always been latent among men in various forms, not only in the civilization of Christendom but wherever and whenever men have had to consider the fundamental problems of life, that is, in every time and place. But it happened to take a particularly concentrated form at this moment in history. It was then the false doctrines we are about to examine stood out in the highest relief and can be most clearly appreciated. By what its effects were when it was thus at its highest point of vitality, we can estimate what evils similar doctrines do whenever they appear.

For this permanent trouble of the human mind has swollen into three great waves during the Christian period, of which three the Albigensian episode was only the central one. The first great wave was the Manichean tendency of the early Christian centuries. The third was the Puritan movement in Europe accompanying the Reformation, and the sequel of that disease, Jansenism. The first strong movement of the sort was exhausted before the end of the eighth century. The second was destroyed when the definite Albigensian movement was rooted out in the thirteenth century. The third, the Puritan wave, is only now declining, after having worked every kind of evil.

Now what is this general tendency or mood which, from its earliest name, was called *Manichean,* which, in its most clearcut form with which we are about to deal, is called the Albigensian, and which we know in modern history as Puritanism? What is the underlying motive power which produces heresies of this kind?

To answer that main question we must consider a prime truth of the Catholic Church itself, which has shortly been put in this form: "The Catholic Church is founded upon the recognition of pain and death." In its more complete form the sentence should rather run "The Catholic Church is rooted in the recognition of suffering and mortality *and her claim to have provided a solution for the problem they present.*" This problem is generally known as "The problem of evil."

How can we call man's destiny glorious and Heaven his goal and his Creator all-good as well as all-powerful, when we find ourselves subject to suffering and to death?

Nearly all young and innocent people are but slightly aware of this problem. How much aware of it they may be depends upon what fortunes they have, how early they may have been brought into the presence of loss by death or how early they may have suffered great physical or even mental pain. But sooner or later every human being who thinks at all, everyone not an idiot, is faced by this *Problem of Evil;* and as we watch the human race trying to think out for itself the meaning of the universe, or accepting revelation thereon, or following warped and false partial religions and philosophies, we find it always at heart concerned with that insistent question: *"Why should we suffer? Why should we die?"*

Various ways out of the torturing enigma have been proposed. The simplest and basest is not to face it at all; to turn one's eyes away from suffering and death; to pretend they are not there, or, when they are thrust upon us so insistently that we cannot keep up the pretense, why then to hide our feelings. And it is part also of this worst method of dealing with the problem to boycott mention of evil and suffering and try to forget them as much as one can.

Another way less base, but equally contemptible intellectually, is to say there is no problem because we are all part of a meaningless dead thing with no creative god behind it: to say there is no reality in right and wrong or in the conception of beatitude or of misery.

Another nobler way, which was the favorite way of the high pagan civilization from which we sprang—the way of the great Romans and the great Greeks—is the way of Stoicism. This might vulgarly be termed "The philosophy of grin-and-bear-it." It has been called by some academic person or other "The permanent religion of humanity," but it is indeed nothing of the sort; for it is not a religion at all. It has at least the nobility of facing facts, but it proposes no solution. It is utterly negative.

Another way is the profound but despairing way of Asia—of which the greatest example is Buddhism: the philosophy which calls the individual an illusion, bids us get rid of the desire for immortality and look forward to being merged in the impersonal life of the universe.

What the Catholic solution is we all know. Not that the Catholic Church has proposed a complete solution of the mystery of evil, for it has never been either the claim or the function of the Church to explain the whole nature of all things, but rather to save souls. But the Catholic Church has on this particular problem a very definite answer within the field of her own action. She says *first* that man's nature is immortal, and made for beatitude; *next* that mortality and pain are the result of his fall, that is, of his rebellion against the will of God. She says that since the fall our mortal life is an ordeal or test, according to our behavior in which we regain (but through the merits of our Saviour) that immortal beatitude which we had lost.

Now the Manichean was so overwhelmed by the experience or prospect of suffering and by the appalling fact that his nature was subject to mortality, that he took refuge in denying the omnipotent goodness of a Creator. He said that evil was at work in the universe just as much as good; the two principles were always fighting as equals one against the other. Man was subject to the one just as much as to the other. If he could struggle at all, he should struggle to join the good principle and to avoid the power of the bad principle, but he must treat evil as an all-powerful thing. The Manichean recognized an evil god as well as a good god, and he attuned his mind to that appalling conception.

Such a mood bred all sorts of secondary effects. In some men it would lead to devil worship, in many more to magic, that is a dependence on something other than one's own free will, to tricks by which we might stave off the evil power or cheat it. It also led, paradoxically enough, to the doing of a great deal of evil deliberately, and saying either that it could not be helped or that it did not matter, because we were in any case under the thrall of a thing quite as strong as the power for good and we might as well act accordingly.

But one thing the Manichean of every shade has always felt, and that is, that *matter* belongs to the evil side of things. Though there may be plenty of evil of a spiritual kind, yet good must be *wholly* spiritual. That is something you find not only in the early Manichean, not only in the Albigensian of the Middle Ages, but even in the most modern of the remaining Puritans. It seems indissolubly connected with the Manichean temper in every form. Matter is subject to decay and is therefore evil. Our bodies are evil. Their appetites are evil. This idea ramifies into all sorts of absurd details. Wine is evil. Pretty well any physical pleasure, or half-physical pleasure, is evil. Joy is evil. Beauty is evil. Amusements are evil—and so on. Anyone who will read the details of the Albigensian story will be struck over and over again by the singularly modern attitude of these ancient heretics, because they had the same root as the Puritans who still, unhappily, survive among us.

Hence derive the main lines which were completed in detail as the Albigensian movement spread. Our bodies are material, they decay and die. Therefore it was the evil god that made the human body, while the good god made the soul. Hence also Our Lord was only *apparently* clothed with a human body. He only *apparently* suffered. Hence also the denial of the resurrection.

Because the Catholic Church was strongly at issue with an attitude of this kind there has always been irreconcilable conflict between it and the Manichean or Puritan, and that conflict was never more violent than in the form it took between the Albigensians and the organized Catholic Church of their day (the eleventh and twelfth centuries) in the west of Europe. The Papacy, the hierarchy and the whole body of Catholic doctrine and established Catholic sacraments, were the target of the Albigensian offensive.

The Manichean business, whenever it appears in history, appears as do certain epidemic diseases of the human body. It comes, you hardly know whence. It is found cropping up in various centers, increases in power and becomes at last a sort of devastating plague. So it was with the great Albigensian Fury of 800 and 900 years ago. Its origins are therefore obscure, but we can trace them.

The eleventh century, the years between 1000 and 1100, may be called the awakening of Europe. Our civilization had just passed through fearful trials. The West had been harried, and in some places Christendom almost extinguished, by droves of pagan pirates from the North, the at first unconverted and later only half-converted Scandinavians. It had been shaken by Mongol raiders from the East, pagans riding in hordes against Europe from the Plains of North Asia. And it had suffered the great Mohammedan attack upon the Mediterranean, which attack had succeeded in occupying nearly all Spain, had permanently subdued North Africa and Syria and threatened Asia Minor and Constantinople.

Europe had been under siege, but had begun to beat off its enemies. The Northern pirates were beaten and tamed. The newly civilized Germans[6] attacked the Mongols and saved the Upper Danube and a borderland to the east. The Christian Slavs organized themselves farther east again. There were the beginnings of the kingdom of Poland. But the main battleground was Spain. There, during this eleventh century, the Mohammedan power was beaten back from one fluctuating border to another further south, until long before the eleventh century was over the great bulk of the Peninsula was recaptured for Christian rule. With this material success there went, and was a cause as well as an effect, a strong awakening of the intelligence in philosophical disputation and in new speculations on physical science. One of those periods had begun which appear from time to time in the story of our race, when there is, so to speak, "spring in the air." Philosophy grew vigorous, architecture enlarged, society began to be more organized and the civil and ecclesiastical authorities to extend and codify their powers.

All this new vitality was working for vigor in heresy as well as in orthodoxy. There began to appear from the East, cropping up now here, now there, but in general along lines of advance towards the West, individuals or small communities who proposed and propagated a new and, as they called it, a purified form of religion.

These communities had some strength in the Balkans, apparently before they appeared in Italy. They seem to have acquired some strength in North Italy before they appeared in France, although it was in France that the last main struggle was to take place. They were known by various names; Paulicians, for instance, or a name referring them to a Bulgarian origin. They were very generally known as "The Pure Ones." They them-

---

6. All Southern Germany had been affected by Roman civilization in some degree, and the Rhine valley most fully. But the final civilization of the Germans as a whole, including the North and the men of the Elbe, was the work of the Catholic missionaries in the early Middle Ages, mainly English and Irish.

selves liked to give themselves that epithet, putting it in the Greek form and calling themselves "Cathari." The whole story of this obscure advance of peril from the east of Europe has been so lost in the succeeding blaze of glory when, during the thirteenth century, Christendom rose to the summit of its civilization, that the Albigensian origins are forgotten and their obscurity is accentuated by the shade which that later glory throws them into. Yet it was an influence both widespread and perilous, and there was a moment when it looked as though it was going to undermine us altogether.

Church Councils were early aware of what was going on, but the thing was very difficult to define and seize. At Arras, in Flanders, as early as 1025, a Council condemned certain heretical propositions of the kind. In the middle of the century again, in 1049, there was another more general condemnation issued by a Council held at Rheims, in Champagne.

The whole influence hung like a miasma or poisonous mist, which moves over the face of a broad valley and settles now here, now there. It began to concentrate and take strong form in southern France, and that was where the final and decisive clash between it and the organized force of Catholic Europe was to take place.

The heresy was helped on its way to definition and strength by the effect of the first great crusading march, which stirred up all Europe and let in a flood of new influences from the East as well as stimulating every kind of activity in the West. That march, as we have seen on a previous page, coincided with the very end of the eleventh century. Jerusalem was captured in 1099. It was with the succeeding century, the twelfth (A.D. 1100-1200), that its effect was manifest. It was a time already greatly in advance of its predecessors. The universities were coming into being, so were representative bodies called parliaments, and the first of the pointed arches arose, the "Gothic." All the true Middle Ages began to appear above ground. In such an atmosphere of vigor and growth the Cathari strengthened themselves, as did all the other forces around them. It was in the early part of this twelfth century that the thing began to get alarming, and already before the middle of the period the northern French were urging the Papacy to act.

Pope Eugenius sent a legate into southern France to see what could be done, and St. Bernard, the great orthodox orator of that vital period, preached against them. But no force was used. There was not any true organization arranged to meet the heretics, although already, far-seeing men were demanding a vigorous action if society were to be saved. At last the peril became alarming. In 1163 a great Church Council held at Tours fixed a label and a name whereby the thing was to be known. Albigensian was that name, and it has been kept ever since.

It is a misleading title. The Albigensian district (known in French as "Albigeois") is practically the same as the department of Tarn, in the central French mountains: a district the capital of which is the town of Albi. No doubt certain of the heretic missionaries had come from there and had suggested this name, but the strength of the movement was not up here in the ill-populated hills, but down in the wealthy plains towards the Mediterranean, in what was called the *Langue d'Oc,* a wide district of which the great city of Toulouse was the capital. Already—a score of years before this Council of Tours had fixed a label and a name on the now subversive movement—Peter of Bruys had been preaching the new doctrines in the *Langue d'Oc,* and with him a companion called Henry had wandered about preaching them at Lausanne, in what is today Switzerland, and later in Le Mans in northern France. It is to be noted that the population were so exasperated with the first of these men that they seized him and burnt him alive.

But as yet there was no official action against the "Albigensians," and they were still allowed to develop their strength rapidly for years on years in the hope that spiritual weapons would be enough to meet them. The Papacy was always hoping against hope that there would be a peaceful solution. In 1167 came a turning point. The Albigensians, now fully organized as a counter-church (much as Calvinism was organized as a counter-church four hundred years later), held a general council of their own at Toulouse and by this time the ominous political fact appeared that the greater part of the small nobles, who formed the mass of the fighting power in the center of France and the south, lords of single villages, were in favor of the new movement. Western Europe in those days was not organized as it is now in great centralized nations. It was what is called "feudal." Lords of small districts were grouped under overlords, these again under very powerful local men who were the heads of loosely joined, but nonetheless unified, provinces. A Duke of Normandy, a Count of Toulouse, a Count of Provence, was in reality a local sovereign. He owed deference and fealty to the King of France, but nothing more.

Now the mass of the smaller lords in the south favored the movement, as many another heretical movement has been favored since by the same class of men, because they saw a chance of private gain at the expense of the Church's landed estates. That had always been the main motive in these revolts. But there was another motive, which was the growing jealousy felt in the south of France against the spirit and character of northern France. There was a difference in speech and a difference in character between the two halves of what was nominally the one French monarchy. The northern French began to clamor again for the suppression of the southern heresy, and thus fanned the flame. At last, in 1194, after Jerusalem had been lost, and the Third Crusade had failed to recover it, the thing came to a head. The Count of Toulouse, the local monarch, in that year took sides with the heretics. The great Pope, Innocent III, at last began to move. It was high time: indeed, it was almost too late. The Papacy had advised delay in a lingering hope of attaining spiritual peace by preaching and example: but the only result of the delay was that it allowed the evil to grow to dimensions in which it imperilled all our culture.

How much that culture was imperilled can be seen from the main tenets which were openly preached and acted upon. All the sacraments were abandoned. In their place a strange ritual was adopted, mixed up with fire worship, called "The Consolation," in which it was professed that the soul was purified. The propagation of mankind was attacked; marriage was condemned, and the leaders of the sect spread all the extravagances which you find hovering round Manicheism or Puritanism wherever it appears. Wine was evil, meat was evil, war was always absolutely wrong, so was capital punishment; but the one unforgivable sin was reconciliation with the Catholic Church. There again the Albigensians were true to type. All heresies make that their chief point.

It was obvious that the thing must come to the decision of arms, for now that the local government of the South was supporting this new highly organized counter-church, if that counter-church grew a little stronger all our civilization would collapse before it. The simplicity of the doctrine, with its dual system of good and evil, with its denial of the Incarnation and of the main Christian mysteries and its anti-sacramentalism, its denunciation of clerical wealth and its local patriotism—all this began to appeal to the masses in the towns as well as to the nobles. Still, Innocent, great Pope though he was, hesitated as every statesmanlike man tends to hesitate before the actual appeal to arms; but even he, just before the end of the century, adumbrated the necessity of a crusade.

When fighting came, it would necessarily be something like a conquest of the southern, or rather south-eastern, corner of France between the Rhone and the mountains, with Toulouse as its capital, by the northern barons.

Still the crusade halted. The turn of the century had passed before Raymond Count of Toulouse (Raymond VI), frightened at the threat from the north, promised to change and withdraw his protection from the subversive movement. He even promised to exile the leaders of the now strongly organized heretical counter-church. But he was not sincere. His sympathies were with his own class in the south, with the mass of fighting men, his supporters, the small lords of the *Langue d'Oc*, who were deep in the new doctrines. St. Dominic, coming out of Spain, became by the force of his character and the directness of his intention, the soul of the approaching reaction. In 1207 the Pope asked the King of France, as sovereign and overlord of Toulouse, to use force. Nearly all the towns of the southeast were already affected. Many were wholly held by the heretics, and when the Papal Legate, Castelnau, was murdered—presumably with the complicity of the Count of Toulouse—the demand for a crusade was repeated and emphasized. Shortly after this murder the fighting began.

The man who stood out as the greatest leader in the campaign was a certain not very important, rather poor lord of a northern manor—a small but fortified place called Montfort, one long day's march on the way to Normandy from Paris.

You may see the ruins of the place still standing in the dense wooded country round about. It lies somewhat to the north of the main road between Paris and Chartres: an abrupt, rather isolated little hill in the midst of tumbled country. To that little isolated and fortified hill the name of "the strong hill," *mont fort,* had been attached, and Simon took his name from that ancestral lordship.

When the fighting began, Raymond of Toulouse was at his wit's end. The King of France was becoming more powerful than he had been. He had recently confiscated the estates and all the overlordship of the Plantagenets in northern France. John, the Plantagenet king of England, French-speaking as was the whole of the English upper class of the day, was also (under the King of France) Lord of Normandy and of Maine and of Anjou, and—through the inheritance of his mother—of half the country south of the Loire: Aquitaine. All the northern part of this vast possession from the Channel right away down to the central mountains had fallen at one blow to the King of France when John of England's peers had condemned him to forfeiture. Raymond of Toulouse dreaded the same fate. But he was still lukewarm. Though he marched with the Crusaders against certain of his own cities in rebellion against the Church, at heart he desired the northerners to be beaten. He had already been excommunicated once. He was excommunicated again at Avignon in 1209, the first year of the main fighting.

That fighting had been very violent. There had been shocking carnage and sack of cities, and there had already appeared the one thing which the Pope most feared: the danger of a financial motive coming in to embitter the already dreadful business. The lords of the north would naturally demand that the estates of the conquered heretics should be carved out among them. There was still an effort at reconciliation, but Raymond of Toulouse, probably despairing of ever being let alone, prepared to resist. In 1207 he was declared an outlaw of the Church, and like John, his possessions were declared forfeited by Feudal law.

The critical moment of the whole campaign came in 1213. It is probable that the forces of the northern French barons would have been too strong for the southerners if Raymond of Toulouse could not get allies. But two years after his final excommunication for forfeiture, very powerful allies suddenly appeared on his side in the field. It seemed certain that the tide would be turned and that the Albigensian cause would win. With its victory the kingdom of France would collapse, and the Catholic Cause in Western Europe. That short group of years, therefore, was decisive for the future. It was in those years that a great coalition, led by the now despoiled John and backed by the Germans, marched against the King of France in the north— and failed. The King of France managed against great odds to win the victory of Bouvines near Lille (29th of August, 1214). But already, the year before, another decisive victory by the Northern Lords in the south against the Albigensians had prepared the way.

The new allies coming to the aid of the Count of Toulouse were the Spaniards from the south side of the Pyrenees, the men of Aragon. There was an enormous host of them led by their king, young Peter of Aragon, the brother-in-law of Raymond of Toulouse. A drunkard, but a man of fearful energy, he was one who was not incompetent at times to conduct a campaign. He led something like one hundred thousand men first and last (a number which includes camp followers) across the mountains directly to the relief of Toulouse.

Muret is a little town to the southwest of Raymond's capital, standing on the Garonne above stream, a day's march from Toulouse itself. The huge Spanish host, which had no direct interest in the heresy itself but a strong interest in weakening the power of the French, was encamped in the flat country to the south of the town of Muret. As against them the only active force available was one thousand men under Simon de Montfort. The odds seemed ridiculous—one to one hundred. It was not nearly as bad as that, of course, because the thousand men were picked, armed, mounted nobles. The mounted forces in the Spanish host were probably not more than three or four times as great, the rest of the Spanish body being footmen, and many of them unorganized. But even so the odds were sufficient to make the result one of the most astonishing things in history.

It was the morning of the 13th of September, 1213. The thousand men on the Catholic side, drawn up in ranks with Simon at their head, heard Mass in the saddle. The Mass was sung by St. Dominic himself. Only the leaders, of course, and a few files could be present in the church itself where all remained mounted, but through the open doors the rest of the small force could watch the Sacrifice. The Mass over, Simon rode out at the head of his little band, took a fetch round to the west and then struck with a sudden charge at the host of Peter, not yet properly drawn up and ill-prepared for the shock. The thousand northern knights of Simon destroyed their enemies altogether. The Aragonese host became a mere cloud of flying men, completely broken up, and no longer in being as a fighting force. Peter himself was killed.

Muret is a name that should always be remembered as one of the decisive battles of the world. Had it failed, the campaign would have failed. Bouvines would probably never have been fought and the chances are that the French monarchy itself would have collapsed, splitting up into feudal classes, independent of any central lord.

It is one of the many distressing things in the teaching of history to note that the capital importance of the place and of the action that was fought there is still hardly recognized. One American author has done it full justice in a most able book: I refer to Mr. Hoffman Nickerson's volume, *The Inquisition.* I know of no other English monograph on this subject, though it ought to be in the forefront of historical teaching. Had Muret been lost, instead of being miraculously won, not only would the French monarchy have been weakened and Bouvines never won, but almost certainly the new heresy would have triumphed. With it our culture of the West would have sunk, hamstrung, to the ground.

For the country over which the Albigensians had power was the wealthiest and the best organized of the West. It had the highest culture, commanded the trade of the Western Mediterranean with the great port of Narbonne, it barred the way of all northern efforts southward, and its example would have been inevitably followed. As it was, the Albigensian resistance collapsed. The northerners had won their campaign, and the South was half-ruined in wealth and weakened in power of revolution against the now powerful central monarchy in Paris. That is why Muret should count with Bouvines as the foundation of that monarchy and with it of the high Middle Ages. Muret opens and seals the thirteenth century—the century of St. Louis, of Edward of England and of all the burgeoning of the occidental culture.

As for the Albigensian heresy itself, it was attacked politically both by civil and by clerical organizations, as well as by arms. The first Inquisition arose from the necessity of extirpating the remnants of the disease. (It is significant that a man pleading his innocence had only to show that he was married to be acquitted of the heresy! It shows what the nature of the heresy was.)

Under the triple blow of loss of wealth, loss of military organization, and a thoroughly organized political rooting out—this Manichean thing seemed in a century to have disappeared. But its roots ran underground, where, through the secret tradition of the persecuted or from the very nature of the Manichean tendency, it was certain to re-arise in other forms. It lurked in the central mountains of France itself and cognate forms lurked in the valleys of the Alps. It is possible to trace a sort of vague continuity between the Albigensian and the later Puritan groups, such as the Vaudois, just as it is possible to trace some sort of connection between the Albigensian and the earlier Manichean heresies. But the main thing, the thing which bore the Albigensian name—the peril which had proved so nearly mortal to Europe—had been destroyed.

It had been destroyed at dreadful cost; a high material civilization had been half ruined and memories of hatred which lingered for generations had been founded. But the price had been worth the paying, for Europe was saved. The family of Toulouse was re-admitted to its titular position, and its possessions did not fall to the French crown until much later. But its ancient independence was gone, and with it the threat to our culture which had so nearly succeeded.

6

WHAT WAS THE REFORMATION?

The movement generally called "The Reformation" deserves a place apart in the story of the great heresies; and that for the following reasons:

1. It was not a particular movement but a general one, *i.e.*, it did not propound a particular heresy which could be debated and exploded, condemned by the authority of the Church, as had hitherto been every other heresy or heretical movement. Nor did it, after the various heretical propositions had been condemned, set up (as had Mohammedanism or the Albigensian movement) a separate religion over against the old orthodoxy. Rather did it create a certain separate *moral atmosphere* which we still call "Protestantism." It produced indeed a crop of heresies, but not *one* heresy—and its characteristic was that all its heresies attained and prolonged a common savor: that which we call "Protestantism" today.

2. Though the immediate fruits of the Reformation decayed, as had those of many other heresies in the past, yet the disruption it had produced remained and the main priciple—reaction against a united spiritual authority—so continued in vigor as both to break up our European civilization in the West and to launch at last a general doubt, spreading more and more widely. None of the older heresies did that, for they were each definite. Each had proposed to supplant or to rival the existing Catholic Church; but the Reformation movement proposed rather to dissolve the Catholic Church—and we know in what measure success has been attained by that effort!

The most important thing about the Reformation is to under-

stand it. Not only to follow the story of it stage by stage—a process always necessary to the understanding of any historical
matter—but to grasp its essential nature.

On this last it is easy for modern people to go wrong, and
especially modern people of the English-speaking world. The
nations we English-speaking people know are, with the exception of Ireland, predominantly Protestant; and yet (with the
exception of Great Britain and South Africa) they harbor large
Catholic minorities.

In that English-speaking world (to which this present writing
is addressed) there is full consciousness of what the Protestant
spirit has been and what it has become in its present modifica-
tion. Every Catholic who lives in that English-speaking world
knows what is meant by the Protestant temper as he knows the
taste of some familiar food or drink or the aspect of some familiar vegetation. In a less degree the large Protestant majorities—in
Great Britain it is an overwhelming Protestant majority—have
some idea of what the Catholic Church is. They know much
less about us than we know about them. That is natural, because
we proceed from older origins, because we are universal while
they are regional and because we hold a definite intellectual
philosophy whereas they possess rather an emotional and
indefinite, though characteristic, spirit.

Still, though they know less about us than we know about
them, they are aware of a distinction and they feel a sharp division between themselves and ourselves.

Now, both Catholics and Protestants today tend to commit a
capital historical error. They tend to regard Catholicism on the
one side, Protestantism on the other, as two mainly opposed religious and moral systems, producing, *from the very origins of
the movement,* opposed and even sharply contrasted moral
characters in their individual members. They take this duality
for granted, even in the beginning. Historians who write in English on either side of the Atlantic talk of so-and-so (even in the
early part of the sixteenth century) as a "Protestant" and so-and-
so-other as a "Catholic." It is true that contemporaries also used
these terms, but they used the words in a very different sense

and with very different feelings. For a whole lifetime after the movement called the "Reformation" had started (say from 1520 to 1600), men remained in an attitude of mind which considered the whole religious quarrel in Christendom as an *Oecumenical* one. They thought of it as a debate in which *all* Christendom was engaged and on which some kind of ultimate decision would be taken for *all*. This decision would apply to Christendom as a whole and produce a general religious peace.

That state of mind lasted, I say, a whole long lifetime—but its general atmosphere lasted much longer. Europe was not resigned to *accept* religious disunion for yet another lifetime. The reluctant resolve to make the best of the disaster does not become evident—as we shall see—till the Peace of Westphalia, 130 years after Luther's first challenge, and the *complete* separation into Catholic and Protestant groups was not accomplished for another fifty years: say, 1690-1700.

It is of first importance to appreciate this historical truth. Only a few of the most bitter or ardent Reformers set out to destroy Catholicism as a separate existing thing of which they were conscious and which they hated. Still less did most of the Reformers set out to erect some other united counter-religion.

They set out (as they themselves put it and as it had been put for a century and a half before the great upheaval) "to reform." They professed to purify the Church and restore it to its original virtues of directness and simplicity. They professed in their various ways (and the various groups of them differed in almost everything except their increasing reaction against unity) to get rid of excrescences, superstitions and historical falsehoods—of which, Heaven knows, there was a multitude for them to attack.

On the other side, during this period of the Reformation, the defense of orthodoxy was occupied, not so much in destroying a specific thing (such as the spirit of Protestantism is today), as in restoring unity. For at least sixty years, even on to eighty years—more than the full active lifetime of even a long-lived man—the two forces at work, Reform and Conservatism, were of this nature: interlocked, each affecting the other and each hoping to become universal at last.

Of course, as time went on, the two parties tended to become two hostile armies, two separate camps, and at last full separation was accomplished. What had been a united Christendom of the West broke into two fragments: the one to be henceforward the Protestant Culture, the other the Catholic Culture. Each henceforward was to know itself and its own spirit as a thing separate from and hostile to the other. Each also grew to associate the new spirit with its own region, or nationality, or City-State: England, Scotland, Hamburg, Zurich and what not.

After the first phase (which covered, naturally enough, about a lifetime) came a second phase covering another lifetime. If one is to reckon right up to the expulsion of the Catholic Stuart kings in England, it covered rather more than a lifetime—close on one hundred years.

In this second phase the two worlds, Protestant and Catholic, are consciously separated and consciously antagonistic one to the other. It is a period filled with a great deal of actual physical fighting: "the Religious Wars" in France and in Ireland, above all in the widespread German-speaking regions of Central Europe. A good deal before this physical struggle was over the two adversaries had "crystallized" into permanent form. Catholic Europe had come to accept as apparently inevitable the loss of what are now the Protestant states and cities. Protestant Europe had lost all hope of permanently affecting with its spirit that part of Europe which had been saved for the Faith. The new state of affairs was fixed by the main treaties that ended the religious wars in Germany (halfway between 1600 and 1700). But the struggle continued sporadically for a good forty years more, and parts of the frontiers between the two regions were still fluctuating even at the end of that extra period. Things did not finally settle down into two permanently separate worlds till 1688 in England, or, even, 1715, if we consider all Europe.

To get the thing clear in our minds, it is well to have fixed dates. We may take as the origin of the open struggle the violent upheaval connected with the name of Martin Luther in 1517. By 1600 the movement as a general European movement had fairly well differentiated itself into a Catholic, as against a Protestant, world, and the fight had become one as to whether the first or the second should predominate, not as to whether the one philosophy or the other should prevail throughout our civilization; although, as I have said, many still hoped that *at last* the old Catholic tradition would die out, or that *at last* Christendom as a whole would return to it.

The second phase begins, say, as late as 1606 in England, or a few years earlier on the Continent and ends at no precise date, but generally speaking, during the last twenty years of the seventeenth century. It ends in France earlier than in England. It ends among the German States—from exhaustion more than for any other reason—even earlier than it ends in France, but one may say that the idea of a direct religious struggle was fading into the idea of a political struggle by 1670 or 1680 or so. The active religious wars filled the first part of this phase, ending in Ireland with the middle of the seventeenth century, and in Germany a few years earlier, but the thing is still thought of as being a religious affair as late as 1688 or even a few years later in those parts where conflict was still maintained.

By the middle of the seventeenth century, in Cromwell's time, 1649-58, Great Britain was definitely Protestant, and would remain so—though possessed of a large Catholic minority.[7] The

---

7. How large this minority was at various dates—1625, 1660, 1685—is debatable, and further confused by the use of similar words for dissimilar things. If we are speaking of the English minority that was actively Catholic in tradition though not fully agreed on Papal claims, people who would have called themselves Catholic rather than Protestant, we have certainly half the population at Elizabeth's death, but only an eighth at the exile of James II eighty-five years later. If we mean all those who would have accepted without hostility a return to the old religion we have, even at the end of 1688, a much larger body. It is difficult to estimate, for men do not leave record of their vaguest opinions, but to say that England still had a one such person in four at that date is no great exaggeration. I have given my reasons in my book on James II.

same was true of Holland. Scandinavia had long been made Protestant for good and all, by her rich men, and so were many Principalities and States of the German Empire, mainly the north. Others (mainly in the south) would clearly be Catholic for the future—in bulk.

Of the Low Countries (what we now call Holland, and Belgium) the north (Holland) with a very large Catholic minority was to be officially Protestant, while the south (Belgium) was to be almost wholly Catholic with hardly any Protestant element at all.

The Swiss Cantons divided, much as the German States did. Some went Catholic, some Protestant. France was to be Catholic, in the main, but with a powerful and wealthy, though not very large, Protestant minority: 10 per cent, at the very most; probably nearer 5 per cent. Spain and Portugal and Italy had settled down to retain for good the traditions of Catholic Culture.

So we are about to follow the story of two successive epochs, gradually changing in character. The first, from a little before 1520 to around 1600, an epoch of universal debate and struggle. The second an epoch of clearly opposed forces, becoming political as much as religious, and more and more sharply defined into hostile camps.

When all this was over, towards the end of the seventeenth century—1700—more than two hundred years ago—there came new developments: the spread of doubt and an anti-Catholic spirit *within the Catholic culture itself;* while within the Protestant culture, where there was less definite doctrine to challenge, there was less internal division but an increasing general feeling that religious differences must be accepted; a feeling which, in a larger and larger number of individuals, grew into the, at first, secret but later avowed attitude of mind that nothing in religion could be certain, and therefore that toleration of all such opinions was reasonable.

Side by side with this development went the political struggle between nations originally of Catholic culture and the regions of the new Protestant culture. During the nineteenth century the preponderance of power gradually fell to the Protestants, led by the two chief anti-Catholic powers, England and Prussia, symbolized sometimes under their capital cities as "London and Berlin." It has been said that "London and Berlin were the twin pillars of Protestant domination during the nineteenth century": and that judgment is sound.

This, then, is the general process we are about to follow. A lifetime of fierce conflict between ideas everywhere; another lifetime of growing regional separation, becoming more and more a political rather than a religious conflict. Then, a century—the eighteenth—of increasing skepticism, beneath which the characteristics of the Catholic and Protestant culture were maintained though hidden. Then another century—the nineteenth—during which the political struggle between the two cultures, Catholic and Protestant, was obvious enough and during which the Protestant culture continually increased its political power at the expense of the Catholic, because the latter was more divided against itself than the former. France, the leading power of Catholic culture, was half of it anti-clerical in Napoleon's day, when England was, as she remains, solidly anti-Catholic.

* * *

The origins of that great movement which shook and split for generations the spiritual world, and which we call the "Reformation," the preparation of the materials for that explosion which shattered Christendom in the sixteenth century, cover two full lifetimes, at least, *before* the first main act of rebellion against religious unity in 1517.

Many have taken as the starting point of the affair the abandonment of Rome by the Papacy and its establishment at Avignon, more than two hundred years before Luther's outbreak.

There is some truth in such an attitude, but it is a very imperfect truth. Everything has a cause, and every cause has another cause behind it, and so on. The abandonment of Rome by the Papacy, soon after 1300, did weaken the structure of the Church but was not in itself fatal. It is better, in seeking the main starting point, to take that awful catastrophe, the plague called today "the Black Death" (1348-50), forty years after the abandonment of Rome. It might even be more satisfactory to take as a starting point the opening of the great schism, nearly thirty years after the Black Death, after which date, for the better part of an active lifetime, the authority of the Catholic world was almost mortally wounded by the struggles of Popes and anti-popes, rival claimants to the awful authority of the Holy See. Anyhow, before the Black Death, 1348-50, and before the opening of the schism, you have to begin with the abandonment of Rome by the Popes.

The Holy See, as the central authority of all Christendom, had long been engaged in a mortal quarrel with the lay power of what was called "The Empire," that is, the Emperors of German origin who had general, but very complicated and varied and often only shadowy, authority, not only in the German-speaking countries, but over northern Italy and a belt of which is now eastern France, as also over the Low Countries and certain groups of the Slavs.

A lifetime before the Popes left Rome this struggle had been coming to a climax under one of the most intelligent and most dangerous men that ever ruled in Christendom, the Emperor Frederick II, whose power was the greater because he had inherited not only the old diversified rule over the German States and the Low Countries and what we call today eastern France, but also eastern and southern Italy. The whole of central Europe, except the States governed immediately by the Pope in the middle of Italy, were more or less under Frederick's shadow, under his claim to power. He challenged the Church. The Papacy won, and the Church was saved; but the Papacy as a political power had become exhausted in the struggle.

As so often happens, a third party benefitted by a violent duel between two others. It was the king of France who now became the chief force, and for seventy years, that is, during all the bulk of the fourteenth century (from 1307 to 1377) the Papacy became a French thing, the Popes residing in Avignon (where their huge palace remains to this day, a splendid monument of that time and its meaning) and the men elected to fill the office of Pope being, after the change, mainly French.

This change (or rather interlude, for the change was not permanent) fell just at the moment when a national spirit was beginning to develop in the various regions of Europe, and particularly in France. All the more did the peculiarly French character of the Papacy shock the conscience of the time. The Papacy ought of its nature to be Universal. That it should be National was shocking to the western European of that time.

The tendency of western Christendom to divide into separate compartments and to lose the full unity which it had possessed for so long was increased by the failure of the Crusades—which as long as they were active had been a unifying force, presenting a common ideal to all Christian chivalry. This tendency was increased also by what is called the Hundred Years War; not that it lasted one hundred years continuously, but that from the first battle to the last you may reckon nearly that space of time.

The Hundred Years War was a struggle between the French-speaking dynasty, ruling in England and supported by the French-speaking upper classes—for all the upper classes in England still spoke French even in the late fourteenth century—and the equally French-speaking monarchy and upper classes in France itself. The English, French-speaking royal family was called *Plantagenet,* and the French royal family we call *Capetian.*

The French Capetian monarchy had descended regularly from father to son for generations until there came a disputed succession after 1300, soon after the Pope went to Avignon in France. The young Edward Plantagenet, the third of that name, the French-speaking King of England, claimed the French crown through his mother, the sister of the last King, who had no son. The Capetian King Philip, cousin of the dead King, claimed as a male, his lawyers inventing a plea that women could neither inherit nor transmit the French monarchy. Edward won two remarkable campaigns, those of Crécy and Poitiers, and nearly succeeded in establishing his claim to be King of France. Then came a long lull in which the Plantagenet forces were driven out of France, save in the southwest. Later came a rally of the Plantagenets, after the usurping Lancastrian branch of that family had made themselves Kings of England, and consolidated their unjust power. They kindled the war in France again (under Henry V of England) and came much nearer to success than their forerunners, because France was in a state of civil war. Indeed, the great soldier of this period, Henry V of England, marrying the daughter of the King of France and saying that her brother was illegitimate, actually succeeded in getting his little son crowned as French King. But the dispute was not over.

We all know how that ended. It ended in the campaigns of Joan of Arc and her successors and the collapse of the Plantagenet claim for good and all. But the struggle had, of course, enhanced national feeling, and every strengthening of the now growing national feeling in Christendom made for the weakening of the old religion.

In the midst of this fell something much more important even than such a struggle, and something which, as I have said above, had most to do with the deplorable splitting up of Christendom into separate independent nations. This woeful incident was the terrible plague, now called "the Black Death." The fearful disaster broke out in 1347 and swept the whole of Europe from east to west. The marvel is that our civilization did not collapse, for certainly one-third of the adult population died, and probably more.

As is always the case in great catastrophes, there was a "time-lag" before the full effects were felt. It was in the 1370's and the 1380's that those effects began to be permanent and pretty much universal.

In the first place, as always happens when men are severely tried, the less fortunate men became violently hostile towards the more fortunate. There were risings and revolutionary movements. Prices were disturbed, there was a snapping of continuity in a host of institutions. The names of the old institutions were kept, but the spirit changed. For instance, the great monasteries of Europe kept their old riches but fell to half their numbers.

The important part of these effects of the Black Death was the appearance of England gradually, after about a lifetime, as a country united by a common tie. The upper classes ceased to talk French, and the various local popular dialects coalesced into a language that was becoming the literary language of a new nation. It is the period of *Piers Ploughman* and of Chaucer.

The Black Death had not only shaken the physical and political structure of European society. It had begun to affect the Faith itself. Horror had bred too much despair.

Another direct result of the Black Death was the "Great Schism" in the Papacy. The warring Kings of France and England and the rival civil factions in France itself and the lesser authorities of the smaller states took sides continually for the one claimant to the Papacy or the other, so that the whole idea of a central spiritual authority was undermined.

The growth of vernacular literatures, that is of literatures no longer generally expressed in Latin, but in the local speech (northern or southern French, or English, or High or Low German) was another disruptive factor. If you had said to a man one hundred years before 1347, "Why should your prayers be in Latin? Why should not our churches use our own language?" your question would have been ridiculed; it would have seemed to have had no meaning. When it was asked of a man in 1447, towards the declining end of the Middle Ages, with the new vernacular languages beginning to flourish, such a question was full of popular appeal.

In the same way opponents of central authority could point to the Papacy as a mere local thing, an Italian, southern thing. The Pope was becoming as much an Italian Prince as he was head of the Church. Such a social chaos was admirably adapted for specific heresies; that is, for particular movements questioning particular doctrines. One very favorite opinion, founded on the social disturbances of the time, was the idea that the right to property and office went with Grace; that authority, political or economic, could not rightly be exercised save by men in a State of Grace—a most convenient excuse for every kind of rebellion!

Grafted on to this quarrel were violent quarrels between the laity and the clergy. The endowments of the Church were very large, and corruption, both in monastic establishments and among the seculars, was increasing. Endowment was beginning to be treated more and more as a revenue to be disposed of for rewards or any political programme. Even one of the best of the Popes of that time, a man fighting the corrupt habit of uniting many endowments in one hand, himself held seven bishoprics as a matter of course.

National and racial feeling took advantage of the confusion in movements like that of the Hussites in Bohemia. Their pretext against the clergy was a demand for the restoration of the cup at Communion to the laity. They were really inspired by the hatred of the Slav against the German. Huss is a hero in Bohemia to this day. During the Great Papal Schism efforts had been made to restore a central authority on a firm basis by the calling of great councils. They called on the Popes to resign. They confirmed new appointments in the Papacy. But in the long run, by shaking the authority of the Holy See, they weakened the idea of authority in general.

After such confusions and such complicated discontents, *particularly the spreading and increasing discontent with the worldliness of the official clergy,* came a vivid intellectual awakening; a recovery of the classics and especially a recovery of the knowledge of Greek. It filled the later fifteenth century—(1450-1500). At the same time the knowledge of the physical world was spreading. The world (as we put it now) was "expanding." Europeans had explored the Atlantic and the African shores, found their way to the Indies round the Cape of Good Hope, and before the end of that century, come upon a whole new world, later to be called America.

Through all this ferment went the continual demand: "Reform of the Church!" "Reform of head and members!" Let the Papacy be recalled to its full spiritual duties and let the corruption of the official Church be purged. There was a rising, stormy cry for simplicity and reality, a rising stormy indignation against the stagnant defense of old privileges, a universal straining against rusted shackles no longer fitted to European society. The cry for change by amendment, for a purification of the clerical body and restoration of spiritual ideals, may be compared to the cry today (centered not on religion, but on economics) which demands a spoliation of concentrated wealth for the advantage of the masses.

The spirit abroad, A.D. 1500-1510, was one in which any incident might produce a sudden upheaval just as the incidents of military defeat, the strain of so many years' warfare, produced the sudden upheaval of Bolshevism in the Russia of our day.

The incident that provoked an explosion was a minor and insignificant one—but as a date of origin it is tremendous. I mean, of course, the protest of Luther against the abuse (and, for that matter, against the use) of indulgences.

That date, the Eve of All Saints, 1517, is not only a definite date to mark the origin of the Reformation, but it is the true initial moment. Thenceforward the tidal wave grew overwhelming. Till that moment the conservative forces, however corrupt, had felt sure of themselves. Very soon after that moment their certitude was gone. The flood had begun.

*　　*　　*

I must here reiterate for purposes of clarity, the very first thing for anyone to realize who wants to understand the religious revolution which ended in what we call today "Protestantism." That revolution, which is generally called "The Reformation," fell into two fairly distinct halves, each corresponding roughly to the length of a human life. Of these the first phase was *not* one of conflict between two religions but a conflict within one religion; while the second phase was one in which a distinct new religious culture was arising, opposed to and separate from the Catholic culture.

The first phase, I repeat (roughly the first lifetime of the affair), was *not* a conflict between "Catholics and Protestants" as we know them now; it was a conflict within the boundaries of one Western European body. Men on the extreme left wing, from Calvin to the Prince Palatine, still thought in terms of "Christendom." James I at his accession, while denouncing the Pope as a three-headed monster, still violently affirmed his right to be of the Church Catholic.

Till we have appreciated that, we cannot understand either the confusion or the intense passions of the time. What began as a sort of spiritual family quarrel and continued as a spiritual civil war, was soon accompanied by an actual civil war in arms. But it was *not* a conflict between a Protestant world and a Catholic world. That came later, and when it came, it produced the state of affairs with which we are all familiar, the division of the white world into two cultures, Catholic and anti-Catholic: the breakup of Christendom by the loss of European unity.

Now the most difficult thing in the world in connection with history, and the rarest of achievement, is the seeing of events as contemporaries saw them, instead of seeing them through the distorting medium of our later knowledge. *We* know what was going to happen; contemporaries did not. The very words used to designate the attitude taken at the beginning of the struggle change their meanings before the struggle has come to an end. So it is with Catholic and Protestant; so it is with the word "Reformation" itself.

The great religious upheaval which so swiftly turned into a religious revolution was envisaged by the contemporaries of its origins as an effort to put right the corruptions, errors and spiritual crimes present in the spiritual body of Christendom. At the beginning of the movement no one worth consideration would have contested for a moment the necessity for reform. All were agreed that things had got into a terrible state and threatened a worse future unless something were done. The crying necessity for putting things right, the clamor for it, had been rising during more than a century and was now, in the second decade of the sixteenth century, come to a head. The situation might be compared to the economic situation today. No one worth consideration today is content with industrial capitalism, which has bred such enormous evils. Those evils increase and threaten to become intolerable. Everyone is agreed that there must be reform and change.

So far so good: You might put it this way: there was no one born between the years 1450-1500 who did not, by the critical date 1517, when the explosion took place, see that something had to be done, and in proportion to their integrity and knowledge were men eager that something *should* be done—just as there is no one alive today, surviving from the generation born between 1870 and 1910, who does not know that something drastic must be done in the economic sphere if we are to save civilization.

A temper of this kind is the preliminary condition of all major reforms, but immediately such reforms proceed to action three characters appear which are the concomitants of all revolutions, and the right management of which alone can prevent catastrophe. The first character is this:

Change of every kind and every degree is proposed simultaneously, from reforms which are manifestly just and necessary—being reversions to the right order of things—to innovations which are criminal and mad.

The second character is that the thing to be reformed necessarily resists. It has accumulated a vast accretion of custom, vested interests, official organization, etc., each of which, even without direct volition, puts a drag on reform.

Thirdly (and this is much the most important character) there appear among the revolutionaries an increasing number *who are not so much concerned to set right the evils which have grown up in the thing to be reformed, as filled with passionate hatred of the thing itself—its essential, its good, that by which it has a right to survive.* Thus today we have in the revolt against industrial capitalism men proposing all at once every kind of remedy—guilds, partial State Socialism, the safeguarding of small property (which is the opposite of Socialism), the repudiation of interest, the debasing of currency, the maintenance of the unemployed, complete Communism, national reform, international reform, even anarchy. All these remedies and a hundred others are being proposed pell-mell, conflicting one with another and producing a chaos of ideas.

In the face of that chaos all the organs of industrial capitalism continue to function, most of them jealously struggling to preserve their lives. The banking system, great interest-bearing loans, proletarian life, the abuse of machinery and the mechanization of society—all these evils go on in spite of the clamor, and more and more take up the attitude of stubborn resistance. They put forward consciously or half-consciously the plea, "If you upset us, there will be a crash. Things may be bad, but it looks as though you were going to make them worse. Order is the first essential of all," etc., etc....

Meanwhile the third element is appearing quite manifestly: the modern world is getting fuller and fuller of men who so hate industrial capitalism that this hatred is the motive of all they do and think. They would rather destroy society than wait for reform, and they propose methods of reform which are worse than the evils to be remedied—they care far more for the killing of their enemy than they do for the life of the world.

All this appeared in what I here call *"The Turmoil,"* which lasted in Europe roughly from 1517 to the end of the century, a lifetime of a little over eighty years. In the beginning all good men with sufficient instruction and many bad men with equally sufficient instruction, a host of ignorant men, and not a few madmen, concentrated upon the evils which had grown up in the religious system of Christendom. Such were the first Reformers.

No one can deny that the evils provoking reform in the Church were deep-rooted and widespread. They threatened the very life of Christendom itself. All who thought at all about what was going on around them realized how perilous things were and how great was the need of reform. Those evils may be classified as follows:

Firstly (and least important) there was a mass of bad history and bad historical habits due to forgetfulness of the past, to lack of knowledge and mere routine. For instance, there was a mass of legend, most of it beautiful, but some of it puerile and half of it false, tacked on to true tradition. There were documents upon which men depended as authoritative which proved to be other than what they pretended to be, for example, the famous false Decretals, and particularly that one called the Donation of Constantine, which, it had been thought, gave its title to the temporal power of the Papacy. There was a mass of false relics, demonstrably false, as for instance (among a thousand others) the false relics of St. Mary Magdalen, and innumerable cases in which two or more competing objects pretended to be the same relic. The list could be extended indefinitely, and the increase of scholarship, the renewed discovery of the past, particularly the study of the original Greek documents, notably the Greek New Testament, made these evils seem intolerable.

The next group of evils was more serious, for it affected the spiritual life of the Church in its essence. It was a sort of "crystallization" (as I have called it elsewhere) or, if the term be preferred, an "ossification" of the clerical body in its habits, and even in doctrinal teaching. Certain customs, harmless in themselves, and perhaps on the whole rather good than otherwise, had come to seem more important, especially as forms of local attachment to local shrines and ceremonies, than the living body of Catholic truth. It was necessary to examine these things and to correct them in all cases, in some to get rid of them altogether.

Thirdly, and much the most important of all, there was worldliness, widespread among the officers of the Church, in the exact theological sense of "worldliness": the preference of temporal interests to eternal.

A prime example of this was the vested interest in Church endowment, which had come to be bought and sold, inherited, cadged for, much as stocks and shares are today. We have seen how, even in the height of the movement, one of the greatest of the reforming Popes held the revenues of seven Bishoprics, thus deprived of their resident pastors. The revenues of a Bishopric could be given as a salary by a King to one who had served him, who never went near his See and lived perhaps hundreds of miles away. It had come to be normal for a man like Wolsey, for example (and he was only one among many others), to hold two of the first-rate Sees of Christendom in his own hand at the same time: York and Winchester. It had become customary for men like Campeggio, learned, virtuous and an example in their lives to all, to draw the revenues of a Bishopric in England while they themselves were Italians living in Italy and rarely approaching their Sees. The Papal Courts, though their evils have been much exaggerated, were recurrent examples, of which the worst was that of Alexander VI's family, a scandal of the first magnitude to all Christendom.

Every kind of man would violently attack such monstrous abuses with the same zeal as men today, both good and bad, attack the wanton luxury of the rich contrasted with the horrible depths of modern proletarian poverty. It was from all this that the turmoil sprang, and as it increased in violence threatened to destroy the Christian Church itself.

Under the impulse of this universal demand for reform, with passions at work both constructive and destructive, it might well have been that the unity of Christendom should have been preserved. There would have been a great deal of wrangling, perhaps some fighting, but the instinct for unity was so strong, the "patriotism" of Christendom was still so living a force everywhere that, like as not, we should have ended by the restoration of Christendom and a new and better era for our civilization as the result of purging worldliness in the hierarchy and the manifold corruptions against which the public conscience was seething.

There was no plan in the air at the beginning of the loud protest during the chaotic revolutionary Lutheran outcry in the Germanies, seconded by the humanist outcry everywhere. There was no concerted attack on the Catholic Faith. Even those who were most instinctively its enemies (Luther himself was not that) and men like Zwingli (who personally hated the central doctrines of the Faith and who led the beginning of the looting of the endowments of religion) could not organize a campaign. There was no constructive doctrine abroad in opposition to the ancient body of doctrine by which our fathers had lived, *until* a man of genius appeared with a book for his instrument, and a violent personal power of reasoning and preaching to achieve his end. This man was a Frenchman, Jean Cauvin (or Calvin), the son of an ecclesiastical official, steward and lawyer to the See of Noyon. After the excommunication of his father for embezzlement and the confiscation by his Bishop of much of the income which he, Jean Calvin, himself enjoyed, he, John, set to work—and a mighty work it was.

It would be unjust to say that the misfortunes of his family and the bitter private money quarrel between himself and the local hierarchy was the main driving force of Calvin's attack. He was already on the revolutionary side in religion; he would perhaps have been in any case a chief figure among those who were for the destruction of the old religion. But whatever his motive, he was certainly the founder of a new religion. For John Calvin it was who set up a counter-Church.

He proved, if ever any man did, the power of logic—the triumph of reason, even when abused, and the victory of intelligence over mere instinct and feeling. He framed a complete new theology, strict and consistent, wherein there was no room for priesthood or sacraments; he launched an attack not anti-clerical, not of a negative kind, but positive, just as Mohammed had done nine hundred years before. He was a true heresiarch, and though his effect in the actual imposition of dogma has not had a much longer life than that of Arianism, yet the spiritual mood he created has lasted on into our day. All that is lively and effective in the Protestant temper still derives from John Calvin.

Though the iron Calvinist affirmations (the core of which was an admission of evil into the Divine nature by the permission of but One Will in the universe) have rusted away, yet his vision of a Moloch God remains; and the coincident Calvinist devotion to material success, the Calvinist antagonism to poverty and humility, survive in full strength. Usury would not be eating up the modern world but for Calvin nor, but for Calvin, would men debase themselves to accept inevitable doom; nor, but for Calvin, would Communism be with us as it is today, nor, but for Calvin, would Scientific Monism dominate as it (till recently) did the modern world, killing the doctrine of miracle and paralyzing Free Will.

This mighty French genius launched his Word nearly twenty years after the religious revolution had begun: round that Word the battle of Church and counter-Church was fought out; and the destruction of Christian unity, which we call the Reformation, was essentially for more than a century to become the product of a vivid effort, enthusiastic as early Islam had been, to replace the ancient Christian thing by Calvin's new creed. It acted as all revolutions do, by the forming of "cells." Groups arose throughout the West, small highly disciplined societies of men, determined to spread "the Gospel," "the Religion"—it had many names. The intensity of the movement grew steadily, especially in France, the country of its founder.

*   *   *

The Reformation, unlike all the other great heresies, led to no conclusion, or at least has led to none which we can as yet register, although the first upheaval is now four hundred years behind us. The Arian business slowly died away; but the Protestant business, though its doctrine has disappeared, has borne permanent fruit. It has divided the white civilization into two opposing cultures, Catholic and anti-Catholic.

But at the outset, before this result was reached, the challenge of the reformers led to fierce civil wars. For the better part of a lifetime it looked as though one side or the other (the traditional, orthodox-rooted Catholic culture of Europe, or the new revolutionary Protestant thing) would certainly prevail. As a fact, neither prevailed. Europe, after that first violent physical conflict, sank back exhausted, registering victory to neither side and formed into those two halves which have ever since divided the Occident. Great Britain, most of north Germany, certain patches of Germans to the south among the Swiss cantons, and even on the Hungarian plain, remained fixed against Catholicism; so did the northern Netherlands, in their ruling part at least.[8] So did Scandinavia. The main part of the Rhine and the Danube valleys, that is, the southern Germans, most of the Hungarians, the Poles, the Italians, the Spaniards, the Irish, and in the main, the French, were found after the shock still clinging to the ancestral religion which had made our great civilization.

To understand the nature of the confusion and general battle which shook Europe is difficult indeed on account of the manifold factors entering into the conflict.

First of all let us fix the chief dates. The active Reformation, the eruption which followed two lifetimes of premonitory shocks and rumblings, broke out in 1517. But fighting between the two opponents did not break out on any considerable scale for forty years. It began in France in 1559. The French religious wars lasted for forty years: *i.e.,* till just on the end of the century. Less than twenty years later the Germans, who had hitherto maintained a precarious balance between the two sides, began *their* religious wars which lasted for thirty years. With the middle of the seventeenth century, *i.e.,* 1648-49, the religious wars in Europe ended in a stalemate.

By 1517 the nations, especially France and England, were already half-conscious of their personalities. They expressed their new patriotism by king-worship. They followed their princes as national leaders, even in religion. Meanwhile the popular languages began to separate nations still more as the common Latin of the Church grew less familiar. The whole modern state was developing and the modern economic structure, and all the while geographical discovery and physical and mathematical science were expanding prodigiously.

In the midst of so many and such great forces all clashing, it is, I say, difficult indeed to follow the battle as a whole, but I think we can grasp it in its very largest lines if we remember certain main points.

---

8. This district—seven out of the 16 Spanish Netherland Provinces, have come to call Holland, after one province alone.

The first is this: that the Protestant movement, which had begun as something merely negative, an indignant revolt against the corruption and worldliness of the official Church, was endowed with a new strength by the creation of Calvinism, twenty years after the upheaval had begun. Though the Lutheran forms of Protestantism covered so great an area, yet the driving power—the center of vitality—in Protestantism was, after Calvin's book had appeared in 1536, Calvin. It is the spirit of Calvin which actively combats Catholicism wherever the struggle is fierce. It is the spirit of Calvin that inhabited dissident sects and that lent violence to the increasing English minority who were in reaction against the Faith.[9]

Now Calvin was a Frenchman. His mind appealed to others indeed, but principally and first to his compatriots; and that is why you find the first outbreak of violence upon French soil. The religious wars, as they are called, which broke out in France, are conducted there with greater ferocity than elsewhere, and even when a halt is called to them, after half a lifetime of horrors, it is a truce and not a victory. The truce was imposed partly by the fatigue of the combatants in France and partly by the Catholic tenacity of the capital, Paris; but it was a truce only.

Meanwhile, religious war had been staved off among the Germans while it had been raging among the French. The turmoil of the Reformation had led at one moment to a social revolution in some German states, but that soon failed, and for a century after the original rebellion of Luther, a long lifetime after the outbreak of religious civil war in France, the Germans escaped general religious conflict in arms.

This was because the Germans had fallen into a sort of tessellated map of free cities, smaller and larger lordships, little states

---

9. A minority till the last years of Elizabeth, but after 1606 an increasing majority opposed the faith because by that time, opposition to the faith had become identified with Patriotism.

and big states. The whole was under the *nominal* sovereignty of the Emperor in Vienna; but the Emperor had neither income nor feudal levies sufficient to impose his personal power. At long last the Emperor, being challenged by a violent Bohemian (that is, Slav) revolt against him, counter-attacked and proposed to re-unite all Germans and impose not only a national unity but a religious unity as well. He would restore Catholicism throughout the German states and their dependencies. He all but succeeded in the attempt. His armies were everywhere' victorious, having for their most vigorous recruitment the Spanish troops, who worked with the Emperor because the Crowns at Madrid and Vienna were in the same family—the Hapsburgs.

But two things came in to prevent the triumph of German Catholicism. The first was the character of a usurping family then reigning over the little Protestant state of Sweden. It had produced a military genius of the first order, the young Swedish King Gustavus Adolphus. The second thing which made all the difference was the diplomatic genius of Richelieu, who in those days directed all the policy of France.

The Spanish power in the south beyond the Pyrenees (backed by all the new-found wealth of the Americas, and governing half Italy), the German power of the empire lying to the east, together threatened France as a nation like the claws of two pincers. Richelieu was a Catholic cardinal. He was personally attached to the Catholic side in Europe, and yet it was he who launched the Protestant military genius, Gustavus Adolphus, against the German Catholic Emperor, with his Catholic Spanish allies, just when victory was in their grasp.

For Richelieu not only discovered the genius of Gustavus Adolphus but discovered a way of hiring that genius. Richelieu had offered him three tubs of gold. He stood out for five—and got them.

Gustavus Adolphus could not have imagined the great future that was in front of him when he took the French gold as a bribe to attempt the difficult adventure of attacking the prestige and power of the Emperor. Like Napoleon and Cromwell and

Alexander and almost all the great captains in history, he discovered his talents as he went along. He must himself have marveled to find how easily and completely he won his great campaigns.

It is an astonishing story. The brilliant victories only lasted a year; at the end of that year Gustavus Adolphus was killed in action at Lutzen, near Leipzig, in 1632, but in so brief a time he very nearly established a Protestant German Empire. He very nearly did what Bismarck was to do two and a half centuries later; even as it was, he made it forever impossible for Germans to be fully united again, and equally impossible for them to return as a whole to the religion of their fathers. He established German Protestantism so firmly that it went on from that day to this increasing in power, until today (from Berlin) it inspires in a new paganized form the great mass of the German peoples.[10]

The religious wars in Germany gradually petered out. By the middle of the seventeenth century, as I have said, a long lifetime after the first fighting had begun in France, there was a general agreement throughout Europe for each party to stand upon its gains, and the religious map of Europe has remained much the same from that day to this, that is from about 1648-49 to our own time.

Now anyone reading only the outward *military* story, with its first chapter of violent French religious war, its second chapter of violent German religious war, would miss the character of the whole thing, though he knew every battle and every leading statesman and warrior; for there underlay that great affair another factor which was neither doctrinal nor dynastic nor international but *moral;* and it was this factor which provoked fighting, imposing peace, and decided the ultimate religious trend of the various communities. It is recognized by historians but never sufficiently emphasized. *It was the factor of greed.*

The old Catholic Europe, prior to Luther's uprising, had been

---

10. What is called "Hitlerism" or "Nazism" today, whatever its future fate, is a despotic and powerful control established by the Prussian spirit over all the Reich.

filled with vast clerical endowments. Rents of land, feudal dues, all manner of incomes, were fixed for the maintenance of bishoprics, cathedral chapters, parish priests, monasteries and nunneries. Not only were there vast incomes, but also endowments (perhaps one-fifth of all the rents of Europe) for every sort of educational establishment, from petty local schools to the great colleges of the universities. There were other endowments for hospitals, others for guilds (that is, trade unions and associations of craftsmen and merchants and shopkeepers), others for Masses and shrines. All this corporate property was either directly connected with the Catholic Church, or so much part of her patronage as to be under peril of loot wherever the Catholic Church was challenged.

The first act of the Reformers, wherever they were successful, was to allow the rich to seize these funds. And the intensity of the fighting everywhere depended upon the determination of those who had looted the Church to keep their loot, and of those who tried to restore the Church to recover the Church wealth.

That is why in England there was so very little fighting. The English people as a whole were little affected in doctrine by the early Reformation, but the monasteries had been dissolved and their property had passed to the lords of the villages and the town merchants. The same is true of many of the Swiss cantons. The French lords of villages, that is the noble class (what are called in England "the Squires,") and the greater nobles above them, were anxious to share in the loot.

The French Crown, dreading the increase of power which this loot would give to the class immediately below it, resisted the movement, hence the French religious wars; while in England a child King and two women succeeding each other on the throne permitted the rich to get away with the Church spoils. Hence the absence of religious wars in England.

It was this universal robbery of the Church, following upon the religious revolution, which gave the period of conflict the character it had.

It would be a great error to think of the loot of the Church as a mere crime of robbers attacking an innocent victim. The Church endowments had come, before the Reformation, to be treated throughout the greater part of Europe as mere property. Men would buy a clerical income for their sons, or they would make provision for a daughter with a rich nunnery. They would give a bishopric to a boy, purchasing a dispensation for his lack of years. They took the revenues of monasteries wholesale to provide incomes for laymen, putting in a *locum-tenens* to do the work of the abbot, and giving him but a pittance, while the bulk of the endowment was paid for life to the layman who had seized it.

Had not these abuses been already universal the subsequent loot would not have taken place. As things were, it did. What had been temporary invasions of monastic incomes in order to provide temporary wealth for laymen became permanent confiscation wherever the Reformation triumphed. Even where bishoprics survived, the mass of their income was taken away, and when the whole thing was over you may say that the Church throughout what remained of Catholic Europe, even including Italy and Spain, had not a half of its old revenues left. In that part of Christendom which had broken away, the new Protestant ministers and bishops, the new schools, the new colleges, the new hospitals, enjoyed not a tenth of what the old endowments had yielded.

To sum up: By the middle of the seventeenth century the religious quarrel in Europe had been at work, most of the time under arms, for over one hundred and thirty years. Men had now settled down to the idea that unity could never be recovered. The economic strength of religion had, in half Europe, disappeared, and in the other half so shrunk that the lay power was everywhere master. Europe had fallen into two cultures, Catholic and Protestant; these two cultures would always be instinctively and directly opposed one to the other (as they still are), but the directly religious issue was dropping out and, in despair of a common religion, men were concerning themselves more with temporal, above all with dynastic and national issues, and with the capture of opportunities for increasing wealth by trade rather than with matters of doctrine.

* * *

After the middle of the seventeenth century, Europe had witnessed the triumph of a Puritan-officered army in England, the triumph of the German Protestants—through the help of France under Cardinal Richelieu—in their effort to shake themselves free from the Catholic control of the Emperor, and the triumph of the Dutch rebels against Catholic Spain. Europe fell back exhausted from the purely religious struggle. The wars of religion were at an end; they had ended in a draw: neither side had won. Religious conflict remained in patches. Thus England tried to kill Catholic Ireland, and France to kill French Huguenotry. But by 1700 it was clear no more national wars of religion would arise.

Henceforward it was taken for granted that our civilization must continue divided. There was to be a Protestant culture side by side with the Catholic culture. Men could not lose the memory of the great past; they did not quickly become what we have since become—nations growing indifferent to the unity of European civilization—but the old moral unity which came of our universal Catholicism was ruined.

Roughly speaking, the mass of Europe fell into the following form:

The Greek or Orthodox Church of the East had ceased to count. Russia had not arisen as a power, and everywhere else the Greek Christians were dominated by, and subject to, Moslems, so that the only map to be considered in 1650 was one stretching from Poland on the east to the Atlantic on the west.

In the region, the Italian peninsula, divided into various states, was wholly Catholic, save for a very small population in some of the northern mountains which had Protestant forms of worship.

The Iberian peninsula—Spain and Portugal—was also wholly Catholic. The Empire, as it was called, that is, the body of states, most of which spoke German and of which the moral head was the Emperor at Vienna, was divided into Protestant states and self-governing cities, and Catholic states and self-governing cities. The Emperor had tried to bring them all back to Catholicism and had failed, because of the diplomacy of Richelieu.

In mere numbers, the Protestant German population was as yet much smaller than the Catholic. Roughly speaking, the northern German states and cities were Protestant and the southern Catholic—not, as is falsely pretended, because something in the northern climate or race tended to Protestantism, but because they lay further away from the center of Catholic power in Vienna. Though the various "Germanies" (as the German-speaking states and cities were called) were thus roughly divided into Protestant North and Catholic South, there were any number of exceptions, islands of Catholic population in the North and Protestant in the South, and often the citizens of one city were divided in religion.

Scandinavia, that is, Denmark, Sweden and Norway, were by this time wholly Protestant. Poland, though it had never formed part of the Roman Empire, went Catholic after a sort of see-saw and hesitation during the time of the religious wars. It has remained one of the most intensely Catholic districts of the world ever since, because, like the Irish, the Poles were violently persecuted for their religion.

The Low Countries had divided into two. The northern provinces (which we now call Holland) had acquired their independence from their original sovereign, the King of Spain, and, largely as a protest against the Spanish power, proclaimed themselves officially Protestant. Their government was Protestant and the political effect of Holland in Europe was Protestant; but it is a great error, though a very common one, to think that the Dutch population as a whole was Protestant. There was a very large Catholic minority and today, of the Christian population—that is the population so declared—over two-fifths but rather less than one-half are Catholic.

The southern provinces of the ancient Netherlands remained solidly of the Catholic culture. They had joined in the revolt against Spain, but when the northern merchants and rich land-owners went Calvinist in order to emphasize the struggle with Spain, the merchants and rich men of the southern provinces reacted strongly the other way. Today we call this Catholic half of the Netherlands Belgium, but it included in the middle of the seventeenth century a strip of what is today French Flanders; for instance, the great town of Lille, the chief city of Flanders, was part of the Catholic and still Spanish Netherlands.

The Swiss Cantons, which were gradually becoming a nation and already mainly independent of the Empire, were divided; some were of the Protestant culture, some of the Catholic—as they remain to this day.

France, after the compromise at the end of the religious wars and the victory of Richelieu over the Huguenots, became offi-cially Catholic. The French monarchy was strongly Catholic and the mass of the nation was of the Catholic culture. But there remained a minority of Protestants, important in numbers (no one knows quite how many, but probably, as we saw on a former page, less than a seventh but more than a tenth of the nation) and far more important in wealth and social position than in numbers. The Protestants in France were also important because they were not confined to one district but were to be found all over the place; for instance, Dieppe, the harbor in the north, was still a strongly Protestant town. So was La Rochelle, the harbor on the Atlantic; so, especially, were many prosperous southern towns such as Montpelier and Nimes. Much of the banking and commerce of France remained in Protestant hands.

England and Scotland in 1650 had been under a common mon-arch for half a century and were both officially Protestant. This English-Scotch monarchy was strongly Protestant, and there was a continual and heavy persecution of Catholicism. But it is another common error to regard the English nation as a whole as being already Protestant at this moment. What was really hap-pening was the dying down of Catholicism very gradually. Per-haps a third of the nation was still vaguely in sympathy with the old religion when the civil wars began, and a sixth of it was willing to make heavy sacrifices by calling itself openly Catholic. Of the officers killed in action on both sides, about one-sixth were estimated to be admittedly and openly Catholics. But it was impossible for the ordinary man to get the Sacraments, and difficult even for rich men, who could afford to pay for private chapels, fines, etc., to get Mass and the Catholic Communion.

Nonetheless, so strong was the ancient root of Catholicism in England that there were constant conversions, especially in the upper classes. For nearly forty years to come it looked as though a very large, solid minority of Catholicism might survive in England, as it had in Holland.

On the other hand, England and Scotland were not only officially Protestant, but a growing majority had come to think of Catholicism as alien to the interests of the country, and a very large and growing minority was filled with a more violent hatred of Catholicism than you could find anywhere else in Europe.

Ireland of course remained Catholic; the number of Protestants present in Ireland, even after the plantations and the conquest by Cromwell, was not one-twentieth of the population. But nineteen-twentieths of the land had been taken by force from the Irish and Catholic people and was now (1650) either in the possession of renegades or of Protestant adventurers from Great Britain, to whom the original owners of the land now had to pay rent or for whom they had to work at a wage.

From this moment, the mid-seventeenth century, when elsewhere there had arisen compromise throughout Europe in the matter of religion, Catholicism was persecuted in Ireland in the most violent fashion, and in a fashion which got more violent as time went on. All the power, very nearly all the land, and most of the liquid wealth of Ireland were in the hands not only of Protestants but of people determined to destroy Catholicism. For a long time to come it was as though Ireland were a test; as though the destruction of the Catholic Church in Ireland were to be a symbol of the triumph of Protestantism and the decline of the Faith. That destruction was nearly accomplished—but not quite.

Such was the map of Europe as the drawn battle of the religious wars had left it.

But apart from the geographical division, the effect of the long struggle, and particularly the fact that it had been inconclusive, was on the moral side more profound than on the geographical.

It was obvious to the eye that European culture would in the future be divided into two camps, but what only gradually entered the mind of Europe was the fact that on account of this permanent division, men were coming to regard religion itself as a secondary thing. Political considerations, the ambition of separate nations and separate dynasties, began to seem more important than the separate religions men professed. It was as though people had said to themselves, not openly, but half-consciously, "Since all this tremendous fight has had no result, the causes which led to the conflict were probably exaggerated."

In the only department that counts, in the mind of man, the effect of the religious wars and their ending in a drawn battle was that religion as a whole was weakened. More and more men began to think in their hearts, "One cannot arrive at the truth in these matters, but we *do* know what worldly prosperity is and what poverty is, and what political power and political weakness are. Religious doctrine belongs to an unseen world which we do not know as thoroughly or in the same way."

That was the prime fruit of the battles not having been won and of the two antagonists virtually consenting to fall back on their positions. There was still plenty of religious fervor on both sides, but in a subtle, undeclared way it was more and more subordinated to worldly motives, especially to patriotism and greed.

Meanwhile, though men did not observe it for a long time, a certain result of this success which Protestantism had obtained, this establishment and entrenching of itself over against the old religion, was working under the surface and was soon to come clearly to light. The Protestant culture, though it remained for another lifetime much smaller numerically than the Catholic culture, and even as a whole poorer, had more vitality. It had begun in a religious revolution; the eagerness of that revolution carried on and inspired it. It had broken up old traditions and bonds which had formed the framework of Catholic society for hundreds of years. The social stuff of Europe was dissolved in the Protestant culture more thoroughly than in the Catholic, and its dissolution released energies which Catholicism had restrained, especially the energy of competition.

All forms of innovation were naturally more favored in the Protestant culture than in the Catholic; both cultures advanced rapidly in the physical sciences, in the colonization of distant lands, in the expansion of Europe throughout the world; but the Protestants were more vigorous in all these than were the Catholics.

To take one example: in the Protestant culture (save where it was remote and simple) the free peasant, protected by ancient customs, declined. He died out because the old customs which supported him against the rich were broken up. Rich men acquired the land; great masses of men formerly owning farms became destitute. The modern proletariat began and the seeds of what we today call Capitalism were sown. We can see now what an evil that was, but at the time it meant that the land was better cultivated. New and more scientific methods were more easily applied by the rich landowners of the new Protestant culture than by the Catholic traditional peasantry; and, competition being unchecked, the former triumphed.

Again, inquiry tended to be more free in the Protestant culture than in the Catholic, because there was no one united authority of doctrine; and though in the long run this was bound to lead to the break-up of philosophy and of all sound thinking, the first effects were stimulating and vitalizing.

But the great, the chief, example of what was happening through the break-up of the old Catholic European unity, was the rise of banking.

Usury was practiced everywhere, but in the Catholic culture it was restricted by law and practiced with difficulty. In the Protestant culture it became a matter of course. The Protestant merchants of Holland led the way in the beginnings of *modern* banking; England followed suit; and that is why the still comparatively small Protestant nations began to acquire formidable economic strength. Their mobile capital and credit kept on increasing compared with their total wealth. The mercantile spirit flourished vigorously among the Dutch and English, and the universal admission of competition continued to favor the growth of the Protestant side of Europe.

All this increase of Protestant power was becoming clear in the lifetime after the Peace of Westphalia (1648-50 to 1720). It was no longer subconscious but conscious, and was felt everywhere as the first third of the eighteenth century progressed. Before the middle of that century there was a feeling in the air that although Catholicism still held the ancient thrones, with all their traditional glory and show of strength—the Imperial Crown, the Papal States, the Spanish Monarchy with its huge dominions overseas, the splendid French Monarchy—yet the future was with the Protestants; Protestantism, to use the modern phrase, was "making good."

Moreover, confidence was on the Protestant side, and the Catholic side was disheartened. One last factor was greatly in favor of the Protestant culture: the decline of religious feeling was going on everywhere after 1750, and this decline of religion did not, *at first,* hurt Protestant society as much as it hurt Catholic society. In Catholic society it divided men bitterly one from the other. The skeptic was there the enemy of his pious fellow-countryman. France, to some extent Italy, much later Spain—but France early in the business—were divided against themselves, while in the Protestant culture difference of opinion and skepticism were commonplaces. Men took them for granted. They led less and less to personal animosities and civil division.

This internal strength the Protestant culture retained on into modern times and has only now begun to lose it, through the gradually disintegrating effect of a false philosophy.

* * *

Rather more than a hundred and fifty years ago, but less than two hundred—say between 1760 and 1770—it should have been clear to any close observer of our civilization that we were entering a period in which the anti-Catholic side of the two halves into which Christendom had split was about to become the chief party. The Protestant culture was about to get the upper hand and would perhaps keep it for a long time. It did, as a fact, not only keep it, but increased its hold for more than a full lifetime—for something like a hundred years. Then—but not till our own times—it declined.

The outward or political signs of this Protestant growth were continued increase of financial, military and naval power on that side of Europe. English commerce rapidly expanded; the Dutch continued to increase their banking and, most important of all, England began to get hold of India. On the military side, the Protestant Germans produced a new and formidable army, that of Prussia, with a strong discipline crowned by victory.

Something that was to have a great effect—the British fleet—became far more powerful than any other, and under its protection English trade and control over the East continually grew. By land Prussia began to win battles and campaigns; these successes of Prussia were not continuous, but they founded a continuous tradition, and her Soldier-King, Frederick II, was certainly one of the great captains of history.

Meanwhile the Catholic culture declined in this same political field.

Austria, that is, the power of the Catholic Emperor among Germans, diminished in strength; so did the vast Spanish Empire, which included at that time much the greater part of populated America.

These material outward signs of increasing Protestant power and the declining power of the Catholic culture were but the effects of a spiritual thing which was going on within. Faith was breaking down.

The Protestant culture was untroubled by this growth of skepticism. The decline of men's adherence to the old doctrines of Christendom did not weaken Protestant society. The whole tone of mind in that society called every man free to judge for himself, and the one thing it repudiated and would not have was the authority of a common religion.

A common religion is of the nature of the Catholic culture, and so the growing decline of belief worked havoc there. It destroyed the moral authority of the Catholic governments, which were closely associated with religion, and it either cast a sort of paralysis over thought and action, as happened in Spain, or, as happened in France, violently divided men into two camps, clerical and anti-clerical.

Still, though we can see what was at work in the eighteenth century, the men of the time did not. England through her sea-power had got a stranglehold on India; Prussia had established herself as a strong power; but no one foresaw that England and Prussia would overshadow Christendom. India was going to produce wealth and power for those who should exploit her and, with her as a base, establish their banking power and commerce throughout the East. Prussia was going to absorb the Germans and overthrow Europe.

England (also through her naval power) had got hold of the French colony of Canada; but no one in those days thought colonies of much importance save as sources of wealth for the mother country, and Canada had never been that for France. Later, when England lost her own colonies in North America and they became independent, it was wrongly regarded as a mortal blow to English power throughout the world.

Very few foresaw what the new republic in North America was going to mean for the future; its vast and rapid expansion in numbers and wealth immensely strengthened the position of the Protestant culture in the world. It was much later that a certain proportion of Catholic immigrants somewhat modified this position, but even so, the United States remained during their astonishing increase an essentially Protestant society.

At the end of the eighteenth century and into the beginning

of the nineteenth came the Revolutionary and Napoleonic wars. These also increased the general strength of Protestantism and still further weakened the Catholic culture. They did so indirectly, and the immediate issues were so much more exciting and so much more directly concerned men's lives that this ultimate and profound effect was little appreciated.

To this day there are very few historians who appreciate the defeat of Napoleon in terms of contrasting cultures in Europe. The French Revolution was an anti-clerical movement, and Napoleon, who was its heir, was not himself a believing and practicing Catholic and cannot be said to have returned to the Faith until his death-bed. Nor, for all his genius, did he clearly perceive that difference of religion is at the root of differences in culture, for the generation to which he belonged had no conception of that profound and universal judgment.

Nevertheless the truth remains that had Napoleon succeeded, the preponderating culture of Europe would have been Catholic. His Empire intermarried with and allied to the ancient Catholic tradition of Austria, giving the Church peace and ending the revolutionary dangers, would have given us a united and settled Europe, where, in spite of the very wide spread of rationalism in the wealthier classes, Europe as a whole would have returned to the Catholic tradition.

Napoleon, however, just failed; and he failed through miscalculating his chances in the campaign in Russia.

After his failure, the process of decline, so long at work in the Catholic culture, continued throughout all the nineteenth century. England, as the result of the defeat of Napoleon, was able to expand uninterruptedly through her now not only unquestioned but invincible sea-power. There was no rival against her anywhere outside Europe. The Spanish Empire, already fallen very low, was broken up, largely through the efforts of England, which desired unimpeded trade with South and Central America. England seized points of vantage all over the globe, some of which became considerable local societies at first called colonies but now "Dominions."

Prussia, through the defeat of Napoleon, became the leading power among the Germans; she annexed the Catholic population of the Rhine and became the triumphant rival of the Hapsburg-Lorraine House, the Emperor at Vienna. France fell into unceasing political experiment and breakdown, at the root of which was the profound religious division between Frenchmen.

There was no united Italy, and such effort as was being made to create one was being made by anti-Catholics. Indeed, it is one of the most amusing ironies of history that the great power which Italy has now become was largely called into being by the sympathy Protestant Europe felt for the original Italian rebellions against the Catholic King of Naples and the authority of the Papal States.

One working lifetime after the defeat of Napoleon another weighty group of events was thrown into the scale against the Catholic culture; this was the series of crushing victories won by Prussia in the field, between 1866 and 1871. In those five years Prussia destroyed the military power of Catholic Austria and created a new German Empire in which the Catholics were carefully cut off from Austria and formed into a minority with Protestant Berlin as their center of gravity. Prussia also suddenly and completely defeated the French Army, took Paris and annexed what suited her of French territory.

This last business, the Franco-Prussian War, was far the most important of all, and might well have proved the end of the Catholic culture in Europe, through the establishment of the Parliamentary French Republic (which went from bad to worse in laws and morals) and from the undermining of the confidence the French had in themselves. The new régime in France began to ruin French civilization and increased indefinitely the anti-Catholic faction, which obtained and kept external power over the French people. Moreover, as a result of that war, England became stronger still in the East, she took the place of France as the master in Egypt, taking over the custody of the Suez Canal (which the French had made just before their final defeat) and acquiring Cyprus.

Italy was now united but weak and despised. Spain and Portugal had declined, it seemed, beyond all hope of recovery; and with France torn by her religious quarrel and having the worst kind of professional politicians in power, with the sun of Austria setting, with Prussia in full career, with the United States now recovering from its Civil War and more powerful and coherent than ever—rapidly becoming the richest country in the world and with a population as rapidly expanding—it seemed a matter of course that the Catholic culture would be beaten right out of the field. The Protestant culture had become the manifest leader of white civilization.

The thing was apparent not only politically, but in the economic field as well. The new machinery which transformed life everywhere, the new rapid communications of thought and goods and men, were mainly the product of the Protestant culture. The nations of Catholic culture did but copy the Protestant nations in these matters.

So it was also with institutions; the English institution of Parliament which had arisen and was maintained under aristocratic conditions by a governing class, was imitated everywhere. It was utterly unsuited to societies with a strong sense of human equality, but such was the prestige of England that men copied English institutions upon every side.

Meanwhile, what may properly be called the test of the fortunes of the Catholic culture, Ireland, seemed to give the signal of that culture's final ruin. The Irish population, long dispossessed of its land, was halved by famine; the wealth of Catholic Ireland fell as rapidly as that of England rose, and no one of consequence thought it possible that Ireland, after her awful experiences in the nineteenth century, could rise again from the dead.

The Pope had been despoiled of his income through the seizure of his States, and was now a prisoner in the Vatican with all the spirit of the new Italian Government, his apparent master, more and more opposed to religion. The educational system of Europe grew more and more divorced from religion, and in the large Catholic countries either broke up or fell wholly into anti-Catholic hands.

* * *

It is very difficult to say when the tide turns in the great processes of history. But one rule may be wisely applied; the turn of the tide comes earlier than men judging by surface phenomena conceive. Any great system—the actively centralized Western Roman Empire, the Spanish Empire, the period of Turkish rule in the East, the period of the absolute Monarchies of Western Europe—has really begun to break down long before the outside observer can note any change. For instance, as late as 1630 men were still talking and thinking of the Spanish power as much the greatest thing in the world; yet it had received its death blow in Holland a lifetime before, and was after Rocroi (1643) slowly bleeding to death.

It was and is so with the Protestant hegemony over our culture, with the Protestant and anti-Catholic leadership of white civilization. The tide has turned. But what was the moment of change? When was "slack water"?

It is difficult to fix a date for these things, but a universal rule is that, in doubt between two dates, the earlier date is to be preferred to the later.

Many would put the years 1899-1901, the ominous Boer War, as the turning point. Some would put it later. For my part, I should fix it round about the years 1885-1887. It seems to me that a universal observer, unbiased by patriotic feeling, would fix that moment—or 1890 at the latest—as the point of flexion in the curve. The Protestant powers were apparently greater than ever; but a reaction was stirring and in the next generation it was bound to become apparent.

Whatever the causes and whatever the precise date to be fixed (certainly somewhere between 1885 and 1904), the tide was turning. It was not turning toward the re-establishment of the Catholic culture as the leader of Europe, let alone to the re-establishment of the Catholic Church as the universal spirit of that culture; but the ideas and the things which had made the opposite culture all-powerful were breaking down. This modern decline of the Protestant hegemony and its succession by an altogether new menace—and a new Catholic reaction against that menace—I shall now describe.

* * *

Whatever date we assign to the summit of power in the Protestant culture, whether we say that its decay was beginning as early as 1890 or that it cannot be put earlier than even 1904,[11] there is no doubt that after this date—in other words, with the very first years of the twentieth century—the supremacy of the Protestant culture was undermined.

The various Protestant heresies upon which it had been based, and the general spirit of all those heresies combined, were declining; therefore their fruit, the Protestant hegemony over Europe and the white world, was declining also. Protestantism was being strangled at its root, at its spiritual root; therefore the material fruits of that tree were beginning to wither.

When we study in detail the process of this veiled decay in the supremacy of the Protestant culture we find two sets of causes. The first, and apparently the least important (though posterity may discover it to be of great importance), was a certain recovery of confidence in a *portion* (but only a portion) of the nations deriving from the Catholic culture, and at the same time a revival of vitality in Catholic teaching.

Politically there was no reaction towards the old strength of the Catholic culture; it was rather the other way. Ireland continued to decline in population and wealth, and was now more subject to a Protestant power than ever before. Poland could apparently no longer hope for resurrection. The divisions within the Catholic culture itself grew worse than ever. In France (which was the keystone of the whole) the quarrel between the Church and her enemies became taken for granted and the vic-

---

11. 1904 was the year of the diplomatic change by which England gave up her age-long alliance with Protestant Prussia and began, with much misgiving and against the grain, to support France.

tory of these enemies taken for granted as well. Religion was dying out in the elementary schools. Great tracts of the peasantry were losing their ancestral faith; and with the decline of religion went a decline of taste in architecture and all the arts—and worst of all in letters. The old French lucidity of thought began to grow confused. There was no revival of Spain, and in Italy, what with anti-clerical and Masonic Parliamentary power and the differences between the various districts, yet another province of Catholic culture grew weaker.

But there was already apparent some revival of religion in the wealthier classes among all the nations of Catholic culture.

This might not seem to mean much, for the wealthier classes are a small minority; but they influenced the universities and therefore the literature and philosophy of their generation. Where, half a lifetime before, anyone would have told you that Catholicism could never again appear in the University of Paris there were evident signs that it was again being taken very seriously. In all this the great Pope Leo XIII played a chief part, seconded by him who was later to become Cardinal Mercier. St. Thomas Aquinas was rehabilitated and the University of Louvain became a focus of intellectual energy radiating throughout Western Europe.

Still, all this was, I repeat, of less significance than the decline of the Protestant culture from within. The Catholic culture continued to be divided; there were no signs of its returning to its great *rôle* in the past; and though the seeds both of Irish and Polish recovery had been sown (the former through the very important recovery of their land by the tenacious Irish peasantry) no one could have foretold—as indeed most cannot yet perceive—the strengthening of the Catholic culture as a whole throughout our civilization.

There were great converts, as there have always been; there were what is even more significant, whole groups of very eminent men, such as Brunetière in France, who grew less and less sympathetic with the old-fashioned atheism and agnosticism, and who, without declaring themselves Catholic, were clearly sympathetic with the Catholic side. But these did not influence the main current; what really made the change was the great internal weakness of the Protestant culture as opposed to the Catholic. It was this decay of the opponent of the Church which began to transform Europe and prepare men for yet another great change, which I shall call (so as to give it a name and be able to study it later) "The Modern Phase."

Protestant culture decayed from within from a number of causes, all probably connected, although it is difficult to trace the connection; all probably proceeding from what physicists call the "auto-toxic" conditions of the Protestant culture. We say that an organism has become "auto-toxic" when it is beginning to poison itself, when it loses vigor in its vital processes and accumulates secretions which continually lessen its energies. Something of this kind was happening to the Protestant culture towards the end of the nineteenth century and the beginning of the twentieth.

This was the general cause of the Protestant decline, but its action was vague and hard to grasp; on the *particular* causes of that decline we may be more concrete and certain.

For one thing, the spiritual basis of Protestantism went to pieces through the breakdown of the Bible as a supreme authority. This breakdown was the result of that very spirit of skeptical inquiry upon which Protestantism had always been based. It had begun by saying, "I deny the authority of the Church: every man must examine the credibility of every doctrine for himself." But it had taken as a prop (illogically enough) the Catholic doctrine of Scriptural inspiration. That great mass of Jewish folklore, poetry and traditional popular history and proverbial wisdom which we call the Old Testament, that body of records of the Early Church which we call the New Testament, the Catholic Church had declared to be divinely inspired. Protestantism (as we all know) turned this very doctrine of the Church against the Church herself, and appealed to the Bible against Catholic authority.

Hence the Bible—Old and New Testaments combined—

became an object of worship in itself throughout the Protestant culture. There was a great deal of doubt and even paganism floating about before the end of the nineteenth century in the nations of Protestant culture; but the mass of their populations, in Germany as in England and Scandinavia, certainly in the United State, anchored themselves to the literal interpretation of the Bible.

Now historical research, research in physical science and research in textual criticism, shook this attitude. The Protestant culture began to go to the other extreme; from having worshipped the very text of the Bible as something immutable and the clear voice of God, it fell to doubting almost everything that the Bible contained.

It questioned the authenticity of the four Gospels, particularly the two written by eyewitnesses to the life of Our Lord and more especially that of St. John, the prime witness to the Incarnation.

It came to deny the historical value of nearly everything in the Old Testament prior to the Babylonian exile; it denied as a matter of course every miracle from cover to cover and every prophecy.

That a document should contain prophecy was taken to prove that it must have been written *after* the event. Every inconvenient text was labelled an interpolation. In fine, when this spirit (which was the very product of Protestantism itself) had done with the Bible—the very foundation of Protestantism—it had left nothing of Protestantism but a mass of ruins.

There was also another example of the spirit of Protestantism destroying its own foundations, but in a different field—that of social economics.

Protestantism had produced free competition permitting usury and destroying the old safeguards of the small man's property— the guild and the village association.

In most places where it was powerful (and especially in England) Protestantism had destroyed the peasantry altogether. It had produced modern industrialism in its capitalistic form; it had produced modern banking, which at last became the master of the community; but not much more than a lifetime's experience of industrial capitalism and of the bankers' usurious power was enough to show that neither the one nor the other could continue. They had bred vast social evils which went from bad to worse, until men, without consciously appreciating the ultimate cause of those evils (which cause is, of course, spiritual and religious) at any rate found the evils unendurable.

But the later wealth and political power of the Protestant culture had been based upon these very institutions, now challenged.

Industrial capitalism and the usurious banking power were the very strength of nineteenth-century Protestant civilization. They had especially triumphed in Victorian England. They are, at the moment in which I write these words, still on the surface all-powerful—but we every one of us know that their hour has struck. They have rotted from within; and with them the Protestant hegemony which they so powerfully supported in the generations immediately before our own.

There was yet another cause of weakening and decline in the Protestant culture: the various parts of it tended to quarrel one with the other. That was what one would have expected from a system at once based upon competition and flattering human pride. The various Protestant societies, notably the British and Prussian, were each convinced of its own complete superiority. But you cannot have two or more superior races. This mood of self-worship necessarily led to conflict between the self-worshippers. They might all combine in despising the Catholic culture, but they could not preserve unity among themselves.

The trouble was made worse by an inherent lack of plan. The Protestant culture having begun by exaggerating the power of human reason, was ending by abandoning human reason. It boasted its dependence upon instinct and even upon good fortune. There was no commoner phrase on the lips of Protestant Englishmen than the phrase, "We are not a logical nation." Each Protestant group was "God's country"—God's favorite—and somehow or other was bound to come out on top without the bother of thinking out a scheme for its own conduct.

Nothing more fatal for an individual or a large society in the long run can be conceived than this blind dependence upon an assured good fortune, and an equally blind neglect of rational processes. It opens the door to every extravagance, material and spiritual; to conceptions of universal dominion, world power and the rest of it, which in their effect are mortal poisons.

All these things combined led to the great breakdown which we date overtly from 1914, but of which the inception lay three years earlier at least; for it was three years before the outbreak of the Great War that the nations began to make their preparations for conflict.

In the Great War, of course, the whole of the old state of affairs went down with a crash. So much as survived what had been the institutions of the Protestant hegemony—control by the banks, the levying of general usury through international loans, the wholly competitive industrial system, the unchecked exploitation of a vast proletariat by a small capitalist class—only survived precariously, propped up by every sort of device, and that in only a few societies. In the mass of our civilization these things rapidly disappeared. The main political institution which had gone with them—parliaments composed of professional politicians and calling themselves "representative"—went down the same road. Our civilization began to enter a period of political experiments, including despotisms, each of which experiments may be and probably is ephemeral, but all of which are, at any rate, a complete break with the immediate past.

The old white world wherein a divided and distracted Catholic culture was overshadowed by a triumphant and powerful Protestant culture was no more.

But let it be noted that this breakdown of the older anti-Catholic thing, the Protestant culture, shows no sign of being followed by an hegemony of the Catholic culture. There is no sign as yet of a reaction towards the domination of Catholic ideas—the full restoration of the Faith by which Europe and all our civilization can alone be saved.

It nearly always happens that when you get rid of one evil

you find yourself faced with another hitherto unsuspected; and so it is now with the breakdown of the Protestant hegemony. We are entering a new phase, "The Modern Phase," as I have called it, in which very different problems face the Eternal Church and a very different enemy will challenge her existence and the salvation of the world which depends upon her. What that modern phase is I shall now attempt to analyze.

7

THE MODERN PHASE

We approach the greatest moment of all.

The Faith is now in the presence not of a particular heresy as in the past—the Arian, the Manichean, the Albigensian, the Mohammedan—nor is it in the presence of a sort of generalized heresy as it was when it had to meet the Protestant revolution from three to four hundred years ago. The enemy which the Faith now has to meet, and which may be called "The Modern Attack," is a wholesale assault upon the fundamentals of the Faith—upon the very existence of the Faith. And the enemy now advancing against us is increasingly conscious of the fact that there can be no question of neutrality. The forces now opposed to the Faith design to *destroy*. The battle is henceforward engaged upon a definite line of cleavage, involving the survival or destruction of the Catholic Church. And *all*—not a portion—of its philosophy.

We know, of course, that the Catholic Church cannot be destroyed. But what we do not know is the extent of the area over which it will survive; its power of revival or the power of the enemy to push it further and further back on to its last defenses until it may seem as though Anti-Christ had come and the final issue was about to be decided. Of such moment is the struggle immediately before the world.

To many who have no sympathy with Catholicism, who inherit the old Protestant animosity to the Church (although doctrinal Protestantism is now dead) and who think that any attack on the Church must somehow or other be a good thing, the struggle already appears as a coming or present attack on what they call "Christianity."

143

You will find people saying on every side that the Bolshevist movement (for instance) is "definitely anti-Christian"—"opposed to every form of Christianity"—and must be "resisted by all Christians irrespective of the particular Church to which each may belong," and so on.

Speech and writing of this kind are futile because they mean nothing definite. There is no such thing as a religion called "Christianity"—there never has been such a religion.

There is and always has been the Church, and various heresies proceeding from a rejection of some of the Church's doctrines by men who still desire to retain the rest of her teaching and morals. But there never has been and never can be or will be a general Christian religion professed by men who all accept some central important doctrines, while agreeing to differ about others. There has always been, from the beginning, and will always be, the Church, and sundry heresies either doomed to decay, like Mohammedanism, to grow into a separate religion. Of a common Christianity there never has been and never can be a definition, for it has never existed.

There is no essential doctrine such that if we can agree upon it we can agree to differ about the rest: as for instance, to accept immortality but deny the Trinity. A man will call himself a Christian though he denies the unity of the Christian Church; he will call himself a Christian though he denies the presence of Jesus Christ in the Blessed Sacrament; he will cheerfully call himself a Christian though he denies the Incarnation.

No; the quarrel is between the Church and the anti-Church—the Church of God and anti-God—the Church of Christ and Anti-Christ.

The truth is becoming every day so much more obvious that within a few years it will be universally admitted. I do not entitle the modern attack "Anti-Christ"—though in my heart I believe that to be the true term for it: No, I do not give it that name because it would seem for the moment exaggerated. But the name doesn't matter. Whether we call it "The Modern Attack" or "Anti-Christ" it is all one; there is a clear issue now joined between the retention of Catholic morals, tradition and authority on the one side, and the active effort to destroy them on the other. The modern attack will not tolerate us. It will attempt to destroy us. Nor can *we* tolerate *it*. We must attempt to destroy it as being the fully equipped and ardent enemy of the Truth by which men live. The duel is to the death.

Men sometimes call the modern attack "a return to Paganism." That definition is true if we mean by Paganism a denial of Catholic truth: if we mean by Paganism a denial of the Incarnation, of human immortality, of the unity and personality of God, of man's direct responsibility to God, and all that body of thought, feeling, doctrine and culture which is summed up in the word "Catholic," then, and in that sense, the modern attack *is* a return to Paganism.

But there is more than one Paganism. There was a Paganism out of which we all came—the noble, civilized Paganism of Greece and Rome. There was the barbaric Paganism of the outer savage tribes, German, Slavonic and the rest. There is the degraded Paganism of Africa, the alien and despairing Paganism of Asia. Now since, from all of these, it has been found possible to draw men towards the universal Church, any new Paganism rejecting the Church now known would certainly be quite unlike the Paganisms to which the Church was or is unknown.

A man going uphill may be at the same level as another man going downhill; but they are facing different ways and have different destinies. Our world, passing out of the old Paganism of Greece and Rome towards the consummation of Christendom and a Catholic civilization from which we all derive, is the very negation of the same world leaving the light of its ancestral religion and sliding back into the dark.

These things being so, let us examine the Modern Attack—the anti-Christian advance—and distinguish its special nature.

We find, to begin with, that it is at once materialist and superstitious.

There is here a contradiction in reason, but the modern phase, the anti-Christian advance, has abandoned reason. It is concerned with the destruction of the Catholic Church and the civilization proceeding therefrom. It is not troubled by apparent contradictions within its own body so long as the general alliance is one for the ending of all that by which we have hitherto lived. The modern attack is materialist because in its philosophy it considers only material causes. It is superstitious only as a by-product of this state of mind. It nourishes on its surface the silly vagaries of spiritualism, the vulgar nonsense of "Christian Science," and Heaven knows how many other fantasies. But these follies are bred, not from a hunger for religion, but from the same root as that which has made the world materialist—from an inability to understand the prime truth that faith is at the root of knowledge; from thinking that no truth is appreciable save through direct experience.

Thus the spiritualist boasts of his demonstrable manifestations, and his various rivals of their direct clear proofs; but all are agreed that Revelation is to be denied. It has been well remarked that nothing is more striking than the way in which all the modern quasi-religious practices are agreed upon *this*—that Revelation is to be denied.

We may take it then that the new advance against the Church—what will perhaps prove the final advance against the Church, what is at any rate the only modern enemy of consequence—is fundamentally materialist. It is materialist in its reading of history, and above all in its proposals for social reform.

Being Atheist, it is characteristic of the advancing wave that it repudiates the human reason. Such an attitude would seem again to be a contradiction in terms; for if you deny the value of the human reason, if you say that we cannot through our reason arrive at any truth, then not even the affirmation so made can be true. Nothing can be true, and nothing is worth saying. But that great Modern Attack (which is more than a heresy) is indifferent to self-contradiction. It merely affirms. It advances like an animal, counting on strength alone. Indeed, it may be remarked in passing that this may well be the cause of its final defeat; for hitherto reason has always overcome its opponents;

and man is the master of the beast through reason.

Anyhow, there you have the Modern Attack in its main character, materialist, and atheist; and, being atheist, it is necessarily indifferent to truth. For God is Truth.

But there is (as the greatest of the ancient Greeks discovered) a certain indissoluble Trinity of Truth, Beauty and Goodness. You cannot deny or attack one of these three without at the same time denying or attacking both the others. Therefore with the advance of this new and terrible enemy against the Faith and all that civilization which the Faith produces, there is coming not only a contempt for beauty but a hatred of it; and immediately upon the heels of this there appears a contempt and hatred for virtue.

The better dupes, the less vicious converts to the enemy, talk vaguely of "a readjustment, a new world, a new order"; but they do not begin by telling us, as in common reason they should, upon what principles this new order is to be raised. They do not define the end they have in view.

Communism (which is only one manifestation, and probably a passing one, of this Modern Attack) professes to be directed towards a certain good, to wit, the abolition of poverty. But it does not tell you why this should be a good; it does not admit that its scheme is also to destroy other things which are also by the common consent of mankind good; the family, property (which is the guarantee of individual freedom and individual dignity), humor, mercy, and every form of what we consider right living.

Well, give it what name you like, call it as I do here "The Modern Attack," or as I think men will soon have to call it, "Anti-Christ," or call it by the temporary borrowed term of "Bolshevism" (which is only the Russian for "whole hogger"), we know the *thing* well enough. It is *not* the revolt of the oppressed; it is *not* the rising of the proletariat against capital injustice and cruelty; it is something from without, some evil spirit taking advantage of men's distress and of their anger against unjust conditions.

Now that thing is at our gates. Ultimately, of course, it is the fruit of the original break-up of Christendom at the Reformation. It began in the denial of a central authority, it has ended by telling man that he is sufficient to himself, and it has set up everywhere great idols to be worshipped as gods.

It is not only on the Communist side that this appears, it appears also in the organizations opposed to Communism; in the races and nations where mere force is set up in the place of God. These also set up idols to which hideous human sacrifice is paid. By these also justice and the right order of things are denied.

*   *   *

Such is the nature of the battle now engaged—and against such enemies the position of the Catholic Church today seems weak indeed.

But there are certain forces in her favor which may lead, after all, to a reaction, whence the power of the Church over mankind may re-arise.

I shall in my next pages consider what the immediate results may be of this new great idolatry; and in the pages following I shall discuss the main question of all. It is this: whether things point to the Church's becoming an isolated fortress defending itself against great odds, an ark in the midst of a rising flood which, though it does not sink the vessel, covers and destroys all else; or whether the Church shall perhaps be restored to something of her ancient power.

The Modern Attack on the Catholic Church, the most universal that she has suffered since her foundation, has so far progressed that it has already produced social, intellectual and moral forms which combined give it the savor of a religion.

Though this Modern Attack, as I have said, is not a heresy in the old sense of the word, nor a sort of synthesis of heresies having in common a hatred of Faith (such as the Protestant movement was), it is even more profound, and its consequences more devastating than any of these. It is essentially atheist, even when the atheism is not overtly predicted. It regards man as sufficient to himself, prayer as mere self-suggestion and—the fundamental point—God as no more than a figment of the imagination, an image of man's self thrown by man on the universe; a phantasm and no reality.

Among his many wise pronouncements, the reigning Pope uttered one sentence, the profound judgment of which was most striking at the time and has been powerfully confirmed by events ever since. What he said was that whereas the denial of God had been confined in the past to a comparatively small number of intellectuals, *that denial had now gained the multitude and was acting everywhere as a social force.*

This is the modern enemy: this is that rising flood; the greatest and what may prove to be the final struggle between the Church and the world. We must judge it principally by its fruits; and these fruits, though not yet mature, are already apparent. What are those fruits?

First, we are witnessing a revival of slavery, the necessary result of denying free will when that denial goes one step beyond Calvin and denies responsibility to God as well as lack of power in man. The two forms of slavery which are gradually appearing and will as time goes on be more and more matured under the effect of the modern attack upon the Faith, are slavery to the State and slavery to private corporations and individuals.

Terms are used so loosely nowadays; there is such a paralysis in the power of definition, that almost any sentence using current phrases may be misinterpreted. If I were to say, "slavery under capitalism," the word "capitalism" would mean different things to different men. It means to one group of writers (what I must confess it means to me when I use it), "the exploitation of the masses of men still free by a few owners of the means of production, transport and exchange." When the mass of men are dispossessed—own nothing—they become wholly dependent upon the owners; and when those owners are in active competition to lower the cost of production the mass of men whom they exploit not only lack the power to order their own lives, but suffer from want and insecurity as well.

But to another man, the term "capitalism" may mean simply the right to private property; to yet another it means industrial

capitalism working with machines, and contrasted with agricul-
tural production. I repeat, to get any sense into the discussion,
we must have our terms clearly defined.

When the reigning Pope in his Encyclical talked of men
reduced "to a condition not far removed from slavery," he meant
just what has been said above. When the mass of families in
a State are without property, then those who were once citizens
become virtually slaves. The more the State steps in to enforce
conditions of security and sufficiency; the more it regulates
wages, provides compulsory insurance, doctoring, education,
and in general takes over the lives of the wage-earners, for the
benefit of the companies and men employing the wage-earners,
the more is this condition of semi-slavery accentuated. And if
it be continued for, say, three generations, it will become so
thoroughly established as a social habit and frame of mind that
there may be no escape from it in the countries where State
Socialism of this kind has been forged and riveted on the body
politic.

In Europe, England in particular (but many other countries
in a lesser degree) has bound itself to this sytem. Below a certain
level of income a man is guaranteed a bare subsistence should
he be out of employment. It is doled out to him by public officials at the expense of losing human dignity. Every circumstance
of his family life is examined; he is even more in the hands
of these officials when out of employment than in the hands of
his employer when employed. The thing is still in transition:
the mass of men do not yet see to what goal they are tending;
but the neglect of human dignity, the potential, if not actual,
denial of the doctrine of free will, have led by a natural consequence to what are already semi-servile institutions. These will
become fully servile institutions as time goes on.

Now against the evil of wage-slavery there has been long proposed and is now working hard, in actual function, a certain
remedy. The briefest name for it is Communism; this is the second form of slavery: slavery to the State: far more advanced

and thorough than the first form, slavery to the capitalist.

Of modern "wage-slavery" one can only talk by metaphor; the man working at a wage is not fully free as is the man possessed of property; he must do as his master tells him, and when his condition is that not of a minority nor even of a limited majority, but of virtually the whole population except a comparatively small capitalist class, the proportion of real freedom in his life dwindles indeed—yet legally it is there. The employee has not yet fallen to the status of the slave, even in the most highly industrialized communities. His legal status is still that of a citizen. In theory he is still a free man who has contracted with another free man to do a certain amount of work for a certain amount of pay. The man who contracts to pay may or may not be making a profit out of it; the man who contracts to work may or may not receive in wages more than the value of what he produces. But both are technically free.

This first form of social evil produced by the modern spirit is rather a tendency to slavery than actual slavery; you may call it a half-slavery, if you like, where it attaches to vast enterprises—huge factories, monopolist corporations, and so on. But still it is not full slavery.

Now Communism is full slavery. It is the modern enemy working openly, undisguisedly, and at high pressure. Communism denies God, denies the dignity and therefore the freedom of the human soul, and openly enslaves men to what it calls "the State"—but what is in practice a body of favored officials.

Under full Communism there would be no unemployment, just as there is no unemployment in a prison. Under full Communism there would be no distress or poverty, save where the masters of the nation chose to starve men or give them insufficient clothing, or in any other way oppress them. Communism worked honestly by officials devoid of human frailties and devoted to nothing but the good of its slaves, would have certain manifest material advantages as compared with a proletarian wage-system where millions live in semi-starvation, and many millions more in permanent dread thereof. But even if it were administered thus Communism would only produce its benefits through imposing slavery.

These are the first fruits of the Modern Attack on the social side, the first fruits appearing in the region of the social structure. We came, before the Church was founded, out of a pagan social system in which slavery was everywhere, in which the whole structure of society reposed upon the institution of slavery. With the loss of the Faith we return to that institution again.

Next to the social fruit of the Modern Attack on the Catholic Church is the moral fruit, which extends of course over the whole moral nature of man. And throughout this field its business so far has been to undermine every form of restraint imposed by human experience acting through tradition.

I say, "so far," because in many parts of morals this rapid dissolution of the bonds must lead to a reaction; human society cannot co-exist with anarchy; new restraints and new customs will arise. Hence those who would point to the modern breakdown of sexual morals as the chief effect of the Modern Attack on the Catholic Church are probably in error; for it will not have the most permanent results. Some code, some set of morals, must, in the nature of things, arise; even if the old code is on this point destroyed. But there are other evil effects, which may prove more permanent.

Now to find out what these effects may be, we have a guide. We can consider how men of our blood carried on before the Church created Christendom. What we chiefly discover is this:

That in the realm of morals one thing stands out, the unquestioned prevalence of cruelty in the unbaptized world. Cruelty will be the chief fruit in the moral field of the Modern Attack, just as the revival of slavery will be the chief fruit in the social field.

Here the critic may ask whether cruelty were not more the note of Christian men in the past than it is today. Is not all the history of our two thousand years a history of armed conflict, massacre, judicial tortures and horrible executions, the sack of towns, and all the rest of it?

The reply to this objection is that there is a capital distinction between cruelty exceptional, and cruelty the rule. When men apply cruel punishments, depend on physical power to obtain effects, let loose violence in the passions of war, if all this is done in violation of their own accepted morals, it is one thing; if it is done as part of a whole mental attitude taken for granted, it is another.

Therein lies the radical distinction between this new, modern, cruelty and the sporadic cruelty of earlier Christian times. Not cruel vengeance, nor cruelty in excitement, nor cruelty in punishment against acknowledged evil, nor cruelty in repression of what admittedly must be repressed, is the fruit of an evil philosophy; though such things are excesses or sins, they do not come from false doctrine. But the cruelty which accompanies the modern abandonment of our ancestral religion is a cruelty native to the Modern Attack; a cruelty which is part of its philosophy.

The proof lies in this: that men are not shocked at cruelty, but indifferent to it. The abominations of the revolution in Russia, extended to those in Spain, are an example in point. Not only did people on the spot receive the horror with indifference, but distant observers do so. There is no universal cry of indignation, there is no sufficient protest, because there is no longer in force the conception that man as man is something sacred. That same force which ignores human dignity also ignores human suffering.

I say again, the Modern Attack on the Faith will have in the moral field a thousand evil fruits, and of these many are apparent today, but the characteristic one, the one presumably the most permanent, is the institution everywhere of cruelty accompanied by a contempt for justice.

The last category of fruits by which we may judge the character of the Modern Attack consists of the fruits it bears in the field of the intelligence—what it does to human reason.

When the Modern Attack was gathering, a couple of lifetimes ago, while it was still confined to a small number of academic men, the first assault upon reason began. It seemed to make but little progress outside a restricted circle. The plain man and his common-sense (which are the strongholds of reason) were not affected. Today they are.

But reason today is everywhere decried. The ancient process of conviction by argument and proof is replaced by reiterated affirmation; and almost all the terms which were the glory of reason carry with them now an atmosphere of contempt.

See what has happened for instance to the word "logic," to the word "controversy"; note such popular phrases as "No one yet was ever convinced by argument," or again, "Anything may be proved," or "That may be all right in logic, but in practice it is very different." The speech of men is becoming saturated with expressions which everywhere connote contempt for the use of the intelligence.

But the Faith and the use of the intelligence are inextricably bound up. The use of reason is a main part—or rather the foundation—of all inquiry into the highest things. It was precisely because reason was given this divine authority that the Church proclaimed mystery—that is, admitted reason to have its limits. It had to be so, lest the absolute powers ascribed to reason should lead to the exclusion of truths which the reason might accept but could not demonstrate. Reason was limited by mystery only the more to enhance the sovereignty of reason in its own sphere.

When reason is dethroned, not only is Faith dethroned (the two subversions go together), but every moral and legitimate activity of the human soul is dethroned at the same time. There is no God. So the words "God is Truth" which the mind of Christian Europe used as a postulate in all it did, cease to have meaning. None can analyze the rightful authority of government nor set bounds to it. In the absence of reason, political authority reposing on mere force is boundless. And reason is thus made a victim because Humanity itself is what the Modern Attack is destroying in its false religion of humanity. Reason being the crown of man and at the same time his distinguishing mark, the Anarchs march against reason as their principal enemy.

* * *

So the Modern Attack develops and works. What does it presage for the future? That is the practical, the immediate question we all have to face. The attack is by this time sufficiently developed for us to make some calculation of what the next phase may be. What doom will fall on us? Or, again, by what good reaction shall we benefit? On that doubt I will conclude.

The Modern Attack is far more advanced than is generally appreciated. It is always so with great movements in the story of mankind. It is yet another case of a "time-lag." A power upon the eve of victory appears to be but half-way to its goal—even perhaps to be checked. A power in the full spring of its early energy appears to contemporaries to be a small precarious experiment.

The modern attack on the Faith (the latest and most formidable of all) has advanced so far that we can already affirm one all-important point quite clearly: of two things one must happen, one of two results must become definite throughout the modern world. Either the Catholic Church (now rapidly becoming the only place wherein the traditions of civilization are understood and defended) will be reduced by her modern enemies to political impotence, to numerical insignificance, and, so far as public appreciation goes, to silence; *or* the Catholic Church will, in this case as throughout the past, react more strongly against her enemies than her enemies have been able to react against her; she will recover and extend her authority, and rise once more to the leadership of civilization which she made, and will thus recover and restore the world.

In a word, either we of the Faith shall become a small persecuted, neglected island amid mankind, *or* we shall be able to lift at the end of the struggle the old battle-cry, *"Christus Imperat!"*

The normal human conclusion in such conflicts—that one or the other combatant will be overwhelmed and will disappear, cannot be accepted. The Church will not disappear, for the Church is not of mortal stuff; it is the only institution among men not subject to the universal law of mortality. Therefore we say, not that the Church may be wiped out, but that it may be reduced to a small band almost forgotten amid the vast numbers of its opponents and their contempt of the defeated thing.

Neither is the alternative acceptable. For though indeed this great modern movement (which so singularly resembles the advance of Anti-Christ) may be repelled, and may even lose its characteristics and die as Protestantism has died before our very eyes, yet that will not be the end of the conflict. This *may* be the final conflict. There *may* be a dozen more to come, or a hundred. But attack upon the Catholic Church there will always be, and never will the quarrel of men know *complete* unity, peace and high nobility through the *complete* victory of the Faith. For if that were so the World would not be the World nor Jesus Christ at issue with the World.

But though not in their entirety, yet in the main, one of those two fates must come, Catholic or Anti-Christian victory. The Modern Attack is so universal and moving so rapidly that men now very young will surely live to see something like a decision in this great battle.

Certain of the most acute modern observers in the last generation and in this have used their intelligence to discover which way fate should fall. One of the most intelligent of French Catholics, a converted Jew, has written a work to prove (or suggest) that the first of these two possible issues will be our fate. He envisages the last years of the Church on this earth as lived apart. He sees a Church of the future reduced to very few in numbers and left on one side in the general current of the new Paganism. He sees a Church of the future within which there will be intensity of devotion, indeed, but that devotion practiced by one small body, isolated and forgotten in the midst of its fellowmen.

The late Robert Hugh Benson wrote two books, each remarkable and each envisaging one of the opposite possibilities. In the first, *The Lord of the World,* he presents the picture of the Church reduced to a little wandering band, returning as it were to its origins, the Pope at the head of the Twelve—and a conclusion on the Day of Judgment. In the second he envisages the full restoration of the Catholic thing—our civilization re-established, reinvigorated, once more seated and clothed and in its right mind; because in that new culture, though filled with human imperfection, the Church will have recovered her leadership of men and will inform the spirit of society with proportion and beauty once more.

What are the arguments to be advanced on either side? On what grounds should we conclude for a tendency one way or the other?

For the first issue (the dwindling of Catholic influence, the restriction of our numbers and political value to the edge of extinction) there is to be noted the increased ignorance of the world about us, coupled with the loss of those faculties whereby men might appreciate what Catholicism means and take advantage of their salvation. The level of culture, including a sense of the past, sinks visibly. With each decade the level is lower than the last. In that decline, tradition is breaking away and melting like a snow-drift at the end of winter. Great lumps of it fall off at one moment and another, melt, and disappear.

Within our generation the supremacy of the classics has gone. You find men upon every side possessed of power who have forgotten that from which we all came; men, to whom Greek and Latin, the fundamental languages of our civilization, are incomprehensible, or at best curiosities. Old men now living can remember uneasy rebellion against tradition; but young men only perceive for themselves how little there is left against which to rebel, and many fear that before they die the body of tradition will have disappeared.

That the mood of faith has been largely ruined, ruined certainly for the greater part of men, all will admit. So true is this that already a majority (I should affirm it to be a very large majority) do not know what the word *faith* means. For most men who hear it (in connection with religion), it signifies either blind acceptance of irrational statements and of legends which common experience condemns, or a mere inherited habit of mental pictures which have never been tested and which at the first touch of reality dissolve like the dreams they are. The whole vast body of apologetics, the whole science of theology (the Queen exalted above every other science) have for the mass of modern men ceased to be. If you but mention their titles you give an affect of unreality and insignificance.

We have already arrived at this strange pass—that while the Catholic body (which is now already *in practice* a minority even in the white civilization) understands its opponents, her opponents do not understand the Catholic Church.

The historian might draw a parallel between the diminishing pagan body of the fourth and fifth centuries, and the Catholic body of today. The pagans, especially the educated and cultivated pagans, who then lived on in smaller and smaller numbers, knew well the high traditions to which they were attached and understood (although they hated) this new thing, the Church, which had grown up among them and was about to dispossess them. But the Catholics who were to supplant the pagans understood less and less of the pagan mood, neglected its great works of art, and took its gods for demons. So today the ancient religion is respected but ignored.

Those nations which are by tradition anti-Catholic, which were once Protestant and have now no fixed traditions, have been so long in the ascendant that they regard their Catholic opponents as finally beaten. Those nations which had retained the Catholic culture are now in the third generation of anti-Catholic social education. Their institutions may tolerate the Church, but are never in active alliance with it and often in acute hostility.

Judged by all the parallels of history and by the general laws which govern the rise and decay of organisms, one might conclude that the active *rôle* of Catholicism in the things of the world was over; that in the future, perhaps the near future, Catholicism would perish.

The Catholic observer would deny the possibility of the

Church's complete extinction. But he also must follow historical parallels; he also must accept the general laws governing the growth and decay of organisms, and he must tend, in view of all the change that has passed in the mind of man, to draw the tragic conclusion that our civilization, which has already largely ceased to be Christian, will lose its general Christian tone altogether. The future to envisage is a pagan future, and a future pagan with a new and repulsive form of paganism, but nonetheless powerful and omnipresent for all its repulsiveness.

Now on the other side there are considerations less obvious, but appealing strongly to the thoughtful and learned in things past and in experience of human nature.

First of all, there is the fact that all through the centuries the Church has reacted strongly towards her own resurrection in moments of deepest peril.

The Mohammedan struggle was a very close thing; it nearly swamped us; only the armed reaction in Spain, followed by the Crusades, prevented the full triumph of Islam. The onslaught of the barbarian, of the northern pirates, of the Mongol hordes, brought Christendom to within an ace of destruction. Yet the northern pirates were tamed, defeated and baptized by force. The barbarism of the eastern nomads was eventually defeated; very tardily, but not too late to save what could be saved. The movement called the Counter-Reformation met the hitherto triumphant advance of the sixteenth-century heretics. Even the Rationalism of the eighteenth century was, in its own place and time, checked and repelled. It is true that it bred something worse than itself; something from which we now suffer. But there was reaction against it; and that reaction was sufficient to keep the Church alive and even to recover for it elements of power which had been thought lost forever.

Reaction there will always be; and there is about Catholic reaction a certain vitality, a certain way of appearing with unexpected force through new men and new organizations. History and the general law of organic rise and decay lead on their largest lines to the first conclusion, the rapid withering of Catholicism in the world; but observation as applied to the particular case of the Catholic Church does not lead to such a conclusion. The Church seems to have an organic, a native life quite unusual; a mode of being unique, and powers of recrudescence peculiar to herself.

Next, let this very interesting point be noted; the more powerful, the more acute, and the more sensitive minds of our time are clearly inclining toward the Catholic side.

They are of course of their nature a small minority, but they are a minority of a sort very powerful in human affairs. The future is not decided for men by a public vote; it is decided by the growth of ideas. When the few men who can think best and feel most strongly and who have mastery of expression begin to show a novel tendency towards this or that, then this or that bids fair to dominate the future.

Of this new tendency to sympathize with Catholicism—and in the case of strong characters to take the risk, to accept the Faith, and proclaim themselves the defenders of it—there can be no doubt. Even in England, where the traditional feeling against Catholicism is so universal and so strong, and where the whole life of the nation is bound up with hostility to the Faith, the conversions which strike the public eye are continually the conversions of men who lead in thought; and note that for one who openly admits conversion there are ten at least who turn their faces towards the Catholic way, who prefer the Catholic philosophy and its fruit to any others, but who shrink from accepting the heavy sacrifices involved in a public avowal.

Lastly there is this very important and perhaps decisive consideration: *though the social strength of Catholicism, in numbers certainly, and in most other factors as well, is declining throughout the world; the issue, as between Catholicism and the completely new pagan thing (the destruction of all tradition, the breaking with our inheritance), is now clearly marked.*

There is not, as there was even quite a short time ago, a confused and heterogeneous margin or *penumbra* which could talk with confidence of itself under the vague title of "Christian," and speak confidently of some imaginary religion called "Christianity." No. There are today already almost quite distinct and sharing the field between them, soon to be as markedly exposed as black and white, the Catholic Church on one side, and on the other the opponents of what has hitherto been our civilization.

The ranks have lined up as for a battle; and though such clear division does not mean that the one or the other antagonist will conquer, it does mean that a plain issue is defined at last; and in plain issues a good cause, like a bad one, has a better chance than in confusion.

Even the most misguided or the most ignorant of men, talking vaguely of "Churches," are now using a language that rings hollow. The last generation could talk, in Protestant countries at least, of "the Churches." The present generation cannot. There are not many churches; there is one. It is the Catholic Church on the one side and its mortal enemy on the other. The lists are set.

Thus are we now in presence of the most momentous question that has yet been presented to the mind of man. Thus are we placed at a dividing of the ways, upon which the whole future of our race will turn.

If you have enjoyed this book, consider making your next selection from among the following . . .

Visits to the Blessed Sacrament. *St. Alphonsus* 5.00
Moments Divine—Before the Blessed Sacrament. *Reuter* 10.00
Miraculous Images of Our Lady. *Cruz* 21.50
Miraculous Images of Our Lord. *Cruz* 16.50
Raised from the Dead. *Fr. Hebert* 18.50
Love and Service of God, Infinite Love. *Mother Louise Margaret* 15.00
Life and Work of Mother Louise Margaret. *Fr. O'Connell* 15.00
Autobiography of St. Margaret Mary 7.50
Thoughts and Sayings of St. Margaret Mary 6.00
The Voice of the Saints. *Comp. by Francis Johnston* 8.00
The 12 Steps to Holiness and Salvation. *St. Alphonsus* 9.00
The Rosary and the Crisis of Faith. *Cirrincione & Nelson* 2.00
Sin and Its Consequences. *Cardinal Manning* 9.00
St. Francis of Paola. *Simi & Segreti* 9.00
Dialogue of St. Catherine of Siena. *Transl. Algar Thorold* 12.50
Catholic Answer to Jehovah's Witnesses. *D'Angelo* 13.50
Twelve Promises of the Sacred Heart. (100 cards) 5.00
Life of St. Aloysius Gonzaga. *Fr. Meschler* 13.00
The Love of Mary. *D. Roberto* 9.00
Begone Satan. *Fr. Vogl* 4.00
The Prophets and Our Times. *Fr. R. G. Culleton* 15.00
St. Therese, The Little Flower. *John Beevers* 7.50
St. Joseph of Copertino. *Fr. Angelo Pastrovicchi* 8.00
Mary, The Second Eve. *Cardinal Newman* 4.00
Devotion to Infant Jesus of Prague. *Booklet* 1.50
Reign of Christ the King in Public & Private Life. *Davies* 2.00
The Wonder of Guadalupe. *Francis Johnston* 9.00
Apologetics. *Msgr. Paul Glenn* 12.50
Baltimore Catechism No. 1 .... 5.00
Baltimore Catechism No. 2 .... 7.00
Baltimore Catechism No. 3 .... 11.00
An Explanation of the Baltimore Catechism. *Fr. Kinkead* 18.00
Bethlehem. *Fr. Faber* 20.00
Bible History. *Schuster* 16.50
Blessed Eucharist. *Fr. Mueller* 10.00
Catholic Catechism. *Fr. Faerber* 9.00
The Devil. *Fr. Delaporte* 8.50
Dogmatic Theology for the Laity. *Fr. Premm* 21.50
Evidence of Satan in the Modern World. *Cristiani* 14.00
Fifteen Promises of Mary. (100 cards) 5.00
Life of Anne Catherine Emmerich. 2 vols. *Schmoeger* 48.00
Life of the Blessed Virgin Mary. *Emmerich* 18.00
Manual of Practical Devotion to St. Joseph. *Patrignani* 17.50
Prayer to St. Michael. (100 leaflets) 5.00
Prayerbook of Favorite Litanies. *Fr. Hebert* 12.50
Preparation for Death. (Abridged). *St. Alphonsus* 12.00
Purgatory Explained. *Schouppe* 16.50
Purgatory Explained. (pocket, unabr.). *Schouppe* 12.00
Fundamentals of Catholic Dogma. *Ludwig Ott* 27.50
Spiritual Conferences. *Faber* 18.00
Trustful Surrender to Divine Providence. *Bl. Claude* 7.00
Wife, Mother and Mystic. *Bessieres* 10.00
The Agony of Jesus. *Padre Pio* 3.00

Prices subject to change.

Prices subject to change.

At your Bookdealer or direct from the Publisher.
Toll-Free 1-800-437-5876   **Fax 815-226-7770**

Prices subject to change.

ABOUT THE AUTHOR

Hilaire Belloc
1870-1953

The great Hilaire Belloc was likely the most famous and influential Catholic historian of the past two centuries. His rare understanding of the central role of the Catholic Faith in forming Western Civilization—from the time of Christ up to our own—still opens the eyes of many today.

Hilaire Belloc was born in 1870 at La Celle, St. Cloud, France. His father was a distinguished French lawyer; his mother was English. After his father's death, the family moved to England. Hilaire did his military service in France, then returned to Balliol College, Oxford, taking first-class honors in history when he graduated in 1895. It has been said that his ambition was to rewrite the Catholic history of his two fatherlands, France and England. In 1896 he married Elodie Hogan of Napa, California; the marriage was blessed with two sons and two daughters.

During a period of 50 years—until he suffered a stroke in 1946—Hilaire Belloc wrote over a hundred books on history, economics, military science and travel, plus novels and poetry. He also wrote hundreds of magazine and newspaper articles. He served for a time as a member of the English House of Commons and edited a paper called the *Eye-Witness.*

As an historian, Belloc is largely responsible for correcting the once nearly universal *Whig* interpretation of British history, which attributed Britain's greatness to her Anglo-Saxon and Protestant background.

Hilaire Belloc visited the United States several times, giving guest lectures at both Notre Dame and Fordham Universities. Among his most famous books are *The Great Heresies, Survivals and New Arrivals* (something of a sequel to the above), *The Path to Rome, Characters of the Reformation,* and *How the Reformation Happened.* Hilaire Belloc died in 1953, leaving behind a great legacy of insight regarding the true, though largely unrecognized, inspirer of Western Civilization—the Catholic Church.